William P. Treloar

Ludgate Hill

Past and present. A narrative concerning the people, places, legends, and changes

of the great London highway. Second Edition

William P. Treloar

Ludgate Hill

Past and present. A narrative concerning the people, places, legends, and changes of the great London highway. Second Edition

ISBN/EAN: 9783337115579

Printed in Europe, USA, Canada, Australia, Japan

Cover: Foto ©ninafisch / pixelio.de

More available books at **www.hansebooks.com**

LUDGATE HILL:

Past and Present.

A NARRATIVE CONCERNING THE PEOPLE, PLACES, LEGENDS, AND CHANGES OF THE

GREAT LONDON HIGHWAY.

Illustrated with Numerous Engravings.

SECOND EDITION.

London:
HAZELL, WATSON, AND VINEY, Ld.,
1, CREED LANE, E.C.
1892.

To the
RIGHT HONOURABLE DAVID EVANS,
LORD MAYOR OF LONDON.

My Lord Mayor,—

The honour you confer upon me by permitting the Second Edition of this little book to be inscribed to you is gratifying in more than one respect; and I hope I may be excused for saying that the association of your name with the subject of the book itself is, in more than one respect, appropriate.

I am one of those who sincerely appreciate your well-known interest in works of public utility and improvement, and your assiduous and successful endeavours to fulfil the duties that awaited you at every step, which have led to your attainment of the distinguished position that you now occupy.

Instead of contriving to secure the high office of Lord Mayor of London, by relying only on wealth and influence to enter at once upon the preliminary dignities of Sheriff and Alderman, without the education and experience acquired by the humbler work of an ordinary member of the Common Council, you honourably "won your spurs" on the "floor of the Court" by undertaking, at the solicitation of your neighbours, to represent your ward, and by heartily devoting your efforts to the work of adequately accomplishing the duties of the successive offices which in the course of time devolved upon you.

Permit me to say, my Lord Mayor, that the course which you have followed has gained for you the regard and esteem of all those who place the claims of public duty before the advantages of public office.

It seems to be appropriate that this expression of respect and goodwill should be offered in the dedication of a book to a Lord Mayor who is the Alderman of the Ward of Castle Baynard, with some scenes in the history of which the following pages have to deal.

Without saying more, except to repeat my thanks, and to express a sincere hope that your term of office may be distinguished by the happy accomplishment of the work you are so competent to initiate and direct,

I am my Lord Mayor,
Your obedient servant,

W. P. TRELOAR.

PREFACE

TO THE SECOND EDITION.

———◆———

IT is more than ten years since the first edition (of twenty thousand) of this book was issued.

While it was in the press I became a member of the Corporation of the City of London; my chief object in entering upon civic duties being to secure the opportunity for calling attention to the necessity for completing the widening and effectually carrying out the improvements of this important thoroughfare in which I have always taken so much interest.

The favour with which "Ludgate Hill Past and Present' was received, and the fact that the first issue has been long exhausted, might be sufficient reasons for my venturing to republish it, but I am right glad to be able to say that there is a perhaps better reason still.

The improvements and extension to which I refer are practically accomplished, and therefore this chronicle demands the addition of another chapter. A brief retrospect of the proceedings in the Court of Sewers, which marked the vicissitudes of the work now so satisfactorily completed, will, I hope, be interesting and acceptable.

These few prefatory words would be incomplete if I did not take the opportunity of referring with much gratification (not unmingled with deep regret for the loss the citizens and indeed all the inhabitants of London have so recently sustained), to the late Chamberlain of the City, Mr. Benjamin Scott, who in letters addressed to me immediately after the publication of the first edition, in 1881, was good enough to speak in terms of commendation of the book, and to express an opinion that it would be well if every quarter of our ancient city were similarly treated. He also furnished me with some items of information in regard to the Prison of Bridewell, the incarceration there of the so-called "Separatists," or Nonconformists, who were unpolitical Puritans in the time of Elizabeth; and to the maintenance of "Bridewell" at the present day as a place to which stubbornly rebellious and disorderly City apprentices may be committed for short terms of imprisonment.

These memoranda, which I had the honour to receive from so distinguished a scholar and antiquarian, are inserted in their proper places in this edition.

"You will be issuing a second edition some day," he wrote, in a courteous and encouraging letter dated January 26th, 1882; and now, though the recollection is that of "the touch of a vanished hand and the sound of a voice that is still," the words are verified.

W. P. TRELOAR.

LUDGATE HILL, LONDON,
    Jan. 1892.

PREFACE

TO THE FIRST EDITION.

THE following pages are intended as a gossiping, but, it is hoped, an entertaining, and perhaps in some instances an instructive, memorial of one of the great highways of the greatest city in the world. The vast extent and continuous growth of London render it impossible for any writer even to indicate its historical associations and archæological remains, unless he is prepared to produce a large book in several volumes, like that of the late Mr. Charles Knight, or the admirable narrative of *Old and New London* published by Messrs. Cassell, Petter, Galpin and Co. But it is still possible to indulge in a brief and yet inclusive retrospect of the history of one particular street or neighbourhood, and to recall its antiquities, its legendary history, and its social aspects with pleasure and advantage. Whether this result has been achieved in the present volume remains to be seen; but at any rate one who has for many years been associated with the locality and with the prosperity of Ludgate Hill may be excused if he imagines that some of its records cannot fail to interest, not only the indulgent, but the impartial reader.

W. P. TRELOAR.

LUDGATE HILL, LONDON,
    Sept. 1881.

LUDGATE HILL AS IT IS—1881.

Ludgate Hill: Past and Present.

INTRODUCTION.

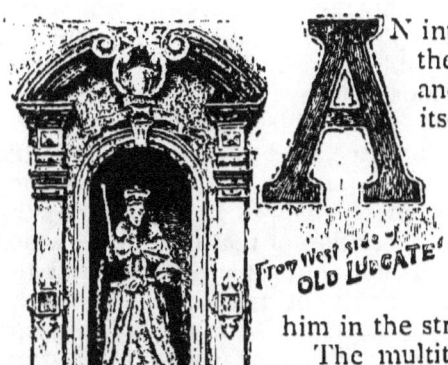

AN intimate acquaintance with the historical highways and byways of London is itself a kind of education. A thoughtful observer who has leisure to loiter and reflect can scarcely tire of the vast field for recollection and speculation which is open to him in the streets.

The multitudinous shops are an endless international and industrial exhibition, where the productions of painters, sculptors, designers, engravers, artificers in gems and precious metals, artists in the making and fashioning of costly fabrics, workmen in wood and stone and iron, and all the manufactures of loom and wheel, are displayed in infinite variety.

On either hand as we pass along we come upon some astonishing example of the application of modern scientific discoveries and inventions, or some stupendous result of mechanical power, amidst surprising transformations, where the old and the new in architecture and in art are blended or contrasted.

But beyond all this, and even in the midst of perpetual change, we are constantly reminded of great historical episodes and exploits, of which there are still so many memorials, not only in public buildings and monuments, but in ancient houses, each with its particular legend, and in the names and titles of streets and localities in which modern improvement and ruthless changes of nomenclature have not erased all historical interest.

All these things make London a perpetual marvel, even to the accustomed wayfarer, and in order truly to appreciate the education afforded by the streets it is necessary to *be* accustomed. They who have learnt the aspects of ancient neighbourhoods, and who know their history—to whom certain houses, doorways, steeples, porches, or even quaint bits of mellowing wall and gable, bear a familiar and friendly aspect, while others are more suggestive of a darker interest, —find in the Great City an unfailing source of pleasure. They will mark with reluctance and regret the inevitable changes that obliterate some records of the past, but they will also remember that these changes are caused by the enormous and continued expansion of that commerce which has been the mainspring of London's prosperity and the occasion of its renown. Even the man of business can spare a few moments of appreciation for the stirring episodes and the venerable memorials of a far-reaching history, which, when rightly understood, is intimately associated with the later developments of human progress.

There is, perhaps, no spot in all wide London where the characteristics to which we have referred are more obvious than in the busy approach to the very core and centre of the world's metropolis—the ascent to the Cathedral of St. Paul—the HILL of LUDGATE.

The Hill is here—and the name, it may be hoped, will never become obsolete. For those who seek them, there are not wanting as many indications of the "old and wide renown" of this great thoroughfare as there are of its present importance. Much of the pomp and circumstance which distinguished it in the days of gorgeous pageants and imposing processions has passed away. It no longer resounds with the clank of arms or the chanting of priests and acolytes; the splendid spectacle of a royal progress scarcely belongs to modern experience; but the mementoes of the vivid events and picturesque shows that distinguished the famous Hill when Lud Gate opened in the City Wall are still numerous, and have formed an appreciable element in the less romantic but perhaps greater "story of our lives from year to year."

Will the reader, to whom this sober introduction may in some sort appeal, give us the pleasure of an hour's good company, and step aside with us, heedless of the passing throng, to a coign of vantage, whence, in brief and simple phrase, we may recall some of the

TRUE LEGENDS OF LUDGATE HILL?

Here is the very place for such discourse, on the rise of the Hill itself. You have but to shut your eyes in a momentary day-dream, and so—vanish the great dreary iron span of the usurping railway bridge at the hill's foot,—vanish the lofty piles of buildings that flank the bridge of Blackfriars;—vanish the bridge itself! There on the right, looming large, is the palace of Bridget's Well, or Bridewell; and across the brawling stream of the Fleet which runs along the valley at the foot of the hill to join the Oldbourne is Fleet Bridge. Looking beyond the intervening space towards the Thames is the church and former Friary of the Dominicans, anciently the seat of the Parliament, and where Wolsey sat with the Pope's Legate; and behind us is the Fleet Prison. On the left is the old Bail Hill and Newgate with its gaol; while further towards St. Paul's the successor of the ancient Lud Gate bestrides the roadway and joins the City Wall, wherein is embedded the prison misnamed a refuge for poor debtors. The great Cathedral is not a church of cupola and dome, but of long nave, broad transept and pointed towers or spires. There, not long ago, the high altar shone resplendent with gold and jewels, and censers swung incense, during high mass, and priests and acolytes crowded the aisles, or waited to show visitors the saintly relics in the shrines.

The tower of Baynard Castle stands upon Thames Bank, where the great navigator, Sir Francis Drake, the foe to Spain, had taken up his abode, while his ship, the *Golden Hind*, lay in the river at Deptford—a grand show, to which the Queen Elizabeth herself has paid a stately visit, and given the knightly accolade to the brave commander.

Still nearer, amidst the huddled streets opposite our standing-place, is Playhouse Yard, and there has been built a new theatre, whither comes one Burbage, from the other theatre—the Globe—on Bankside. He has brought with him a company of players to perform the dramas of Ben Jonson and of one William Shakespeare, of whom not only the Court, but all the town, will soon be talking. This Shakespeare will be here presently, for we have taken our stand beside the deep archway of the old "Bell Savage" Inn (you can see the wide, cool inn-yard beyond, with its tier of upper rooms behind heavy wooden balconies). The guests are even now coming from their rooms, and taking their places on the balconies, to witness the performance of Bankes and his wonderful horse Marocco, and to listen to the jests of the famous clown, Tarleton, who comes from performing at another inn in Grasschurch Street, by London Bridge.

There is a bench here, so let us sit down. It is the seat where rested Sir Thomas Wyatt. But we must tell that story presently—the story of the old Bell Savage—for we must go further backward yet in the chronicles of brick and stone, and have but mentioned Shakespeare and his day as a hint of the kind of company that we shall meet with, and of the place where the legends of Ludgate Hill may be most fitly recalled.*

* The corner of Belle Sauvage Yard, by the spot formerly the outer gateway of the old inn of the Savage family, with the title of "The Bell on the Hoop," and afterwards the "Bell Savage" inn or hostelry. The place is mentioned as early as the reign of Henry VI. in the record of a legal transfer, and was then of some antiquity. The corner now referred to is No. 68, Ludgate Hill, the new establishment of Messrs. Treloar & Sons, who also occupy the premises No. 69, opposite.

Ludgate Hill has been a representative locality from the earliest age from which we can date either records or traditions of London. It was the famous highway of our chronicles, for it was in the midst of noted churches, castles, palaces, courts of ecclesiastical and civil law, hospitals, prisons, priories, theatres, fairs and markets ; and was daily crowded with nobles, priests, knights, mendicant friars, flagellants, pilgrims, men-at-arms, citizens and yeomen ; who visited its shops and stalls, or passed about its narrow streets, many of which led to the mansions of the nobility in various parts of the City between St. Bride's or Holborn and the Tower.

If King Lud did not sit, as it were, enthroned for all time at Lud Gate, at all events he has had the credit of it in popular legend, and with him, therefore, our own veracious chronicle truly begins.

But as with him the inflated exaggerations of the former legend-mongers appear to draw to a close, we must take their praises of his achievements with a very large pinch of salt indeed. That he was a jovial feaster and boon companion is quite probable, and he may have been famous in his day as a warrior, and even as a legislator, so far as these qualities would be exercised by a chief whose brother became historical, and of whom, therefore, we know something definite. It is even possible that he really repaired several old towns and buildings ; but we have to ask ourselves what were the towns and edifices of Britain before the Roman conquest? and above all, what was the old city of "Troynovant" before, as was alleged, Lud enlarged it, surrounded it with a wall of stone, built Lud Gate, and erected a palace which long afterwards became the bishop's palace, and a temple which was the beginning of the Church of St. Paul?

It is impossible to reduce these declarations to any definite proportions, and we are therefore driven to the humiliating confession that though it is also asserted that the name London is derived from Lud Town, which sounds as though somebody with a cold in his head had tried to mention the more modern appellation, and the word Ludgate remains apparently unaltered, there are as many etymological objections to these derivations as there are historical difficulties in the way of assigning to Lud himself a position of such high distinction as the older legends claim for him.

All that we can really yield to the memory of King Lud is that he probably was a person of some importance in his day, and he may have given his name to a town; but Lud

EFFIGIES OF KING LUD AND HIS SONS, ON LUD GATE (*see page* 110).

Town is almost as visionary as Troynovant when we seek in it the derivation of London; and the oldest Lud Gate of the remains of which there is any authentic record, was no older than the reign of King John, and was adorned with sculptured figures purporting to represent Lud and his two sons (who were to succeed him in place of his brother Cassivellaunus), all three in Roman costume, so that if the family had been thus immortalised at any earlier date it must still have been by some artificer to whom their fame had come down by local association.

That there was a town on the site which is now occupied by St. Paul's and its surroundings, and that a heathen temple, perhaps afterwards a Temple of Diana, may have stood there, is by no means improbable; nor is it impossible that the town may have had a gate, though it is exceedingly unlikely that in the time just before the Roman invasion it was surrounded by a stone wall, since the Britons were never known to have walled towns—a fact certainly remarked by Cæsar and never contradicted, even when London was spoken of not long afterwards.

"LONDON."

There is room and verge enough for choosing the derivation of "London" without King Lud, or the *Caer Ludd* of the Welsh fabulists, who, by-the-bye, perhaps meant Caer Floyd or Lloyd; and Troynovant may be no more than the Cornish *Tre* and the Latin *novant*—the New City. Tacitus and other Latin writers call it *Londinium* and *Lundinium*, and it was afterwards named *Augusta*, in compliment to Valentinian, by whom probably the greater part of the wall was built. Bede called it *Lundonia*, which Alfred the Great translated into *Lundenceastre*; and it has been called *Lundene* and *Lundunes*, which come tolerably near to the other Welsh or Celtic British *Llyn Din*, or City on a Lake; or the Belgic-British *Lun-Den*, a Grove City. Then we have *Llawn* (full) and *Dyn* (man), implying a populous place. Camden went for *Llong Dinas*, a City of Ships; and Selden, who thought of the reputed Temple of Diana, ventured to suggest *Llan Dien*.

But the maze of etymologists would seem to be only less hopeless than the flights of fabulists; so there we leave the subject, with a lingering suspicion, however, that our old friend Lud is, to use a modern phrase, "not in it." Nor—grievous as the admission may be—is it by any means certain that his name actually survives in the gate supposed to have been his, except that the coincidence of his real and important historical existence at a period near to that of gate and wall having been built has led to the association. The contention is that it meant Flud or Flood Gate—the Gate on the Fleet or Flood, which was the stream fed by the

LUD GATE.

River of Wells and Turnmill Brook, and running from the Old Bourne, along the bottom of the Hill, to the Thames. But, as Leigh Hunt observes, it is not easy to see in that case why Fleet Street should not have been called Lud Street, and perhaps the old tradition is so far true that some ancient Lud or Lloyd was the builder of an "old original" gate, whether king or not.

In 1669, while the workmen were digging out the ruins after the Fire of London, in the place where the *vallum*, or rampart, of this camp had been, near Ludgate, they came upon a sepulchral monument in memory of Vivius Marcianus, a Roman soldier of the Second Legion, quartered here.* It had been erected by his wife, Januaria Marina, and represented him as a British soldier, probably of the Cohors Britonum, dressed and armed after the manner of the country, in long hair, a short lower garment, fastened round the waist by a girdle and fibula, a long sagum or plaid flung over his breast and one arm, ready to be cast off in time of action, bare legs, and in his right hand a sword of vast length, like the claymore of the later Highlanders. The point of the sword was resting on the ground. In his left hand was what appears to be a portion of a weapon, the end of which is broken.

And here we are met at once by a difficulty. The old Roman wall of London could scarcely have come beyond where the east end of Saint Paul's now stands, unless the Romans there departed from their rule of never permitting a cemetery to be within their cities. They were strict advocates of extra-mural interment, and it might have been better in some respects if their successors had followed their example, though we confess that antiquarians and archæologists would have had less to write about if there had been no tombs in the churches, and the cemeteries had all been reduced to the condition lately presented by Bunhill Fields. It is possible, however, to imagine an outer as well as an inner wall; and, according to the most authentic narrators, the old Roman—or the restored Roman—wall began at a fort which occupied part of the site of the present Tower of London; continuing by the Minories to Aldgate, Bevis Marks, Camomile Street, and Houndsditch, to Bishopsgate, and straight through to Cripplegate; turning to Aldersgate, Newgate, and Ludgate; passing at the back

* The bodies of soldiers were always buried in the *vallum;* those of the citizens in the *pomœrium*, a space outside fortified towns on which all buildings were prohibited.

of the spot not very long ago occupied by the College of Physicians in Warwick Lane; by Stationers' Hall, and so to the gate near St. Martin's Church; crossing Ludgate Hill, and extending down the opposite side westward to the present Ludgate Circus; thence turning southward, and skirting Fleet Brook, to the Thames, where was another tower joining it to the wall that ran along Thames Bank, back again to the Tower; a wall which even Fitz-Stephen, who wrote in the reign of the Second Henry, says "was long since subverted by the *fishful* river."

Comparatively few Saxon relics have been discovered within that area, the circuit of which from the Tower round to the Fleet at the foot of Ludgate Hill was two miles and a furlong, without reckoning that along the river bank. Still fewer are the relics of the ancient Britons. Saxon London was but a small improvement upon the Roman city; indeed, it was Roman London despoiled, but growing yearly richer in the commerce planted by the former invaders, and more enlightened by the Christianity which Augustine had brought to Ethelbert, the builder of the then humble cathedral church of Saint Paul, wherein was placed the shrine of the Saxon saint Erkenwald. It was in digging out the foundations of the stupendous and magnificent cathedral, which had been finished in the reign of Henry III., covering the site of the former poor structure, that the excavators employed by Sir Christopher Wren came upon a large cemetery, wherein first lay the Saxons in graves lined with boulders of chalk or in coffins of hollowed stone. Beneath these were the graves of Britons and of Romans, the latter the deepest, but apparently of the same period, when conquerors and conquered lived and died together in the city. The graves of the Britons contained little but the wooden or bone pins with which the woollen shrouds had been fastened round the dead; in the deeper Roman graves were found funeral urns, lamps, lachrymatories (or tear-phials), and some sacrificial and other glass and earthenware vessels of great beauty of design and colour. The little blocks of jasper, porphyry, and marble belonging to a tesselated pavement were also found, and numerous glass rings and beads, probably belonging to the Britons, as well as boars' tusks and deer-horns half sawn through, and coins of different emperors, including Constantine.

But we must pass that period—the early time of Ludgate and the Hill—and must leave Canute the Dane to make London stronger, and to increase its importance, till the Norman comes to lord it within the walls, and build there palaces, and castles, and bishops' mansions and fairer churches, and to bring the legends and the sports and pastimes of chivalry into the broad streets, with their quaint, low houses of wood, thatched with straw or reeds, and fronted with beams and coloured plaster, overhanging the footways. The great enemy of London in these days is fire, and the wells and brooks and conduits are the chief safeguard, for they are numerous, from the Tower Ditch to Fleet, and from the Clerk's-well to Walbrook and Langbourne. The wide hill of Ludgate is thronged, for the City flourishes, and William King has granted to William Bishop a charter ensuring its wonted liberties and privileges, as they were ordained by Edward King and Confessor. But the castle of the Norman noble dominates all, and the power of feudal rule is seen in tower and portcullis, and pierced battlements;—in processions of proud knights and fighting bishops, in the bravery of caparisoned steed and flaunting pennon, the songs of friars and the chants of monks, the chatter of dames and damsels with flagons and water-pitchers, the clatter of men-at-arms and the thrumming of lutes and bow-strings at the shops by Ludgate in Bowyer Row, where the armourers have their stalls, or by the banks of the Fleet, that runs brawling and foaming in the valley and along by the walls and the water-gate of Bridewell.

The Fleet River.

The Fleet was well named the river of wells at the time we speak of it, for it was a clear and pellucid stream, fit tributary of a fishful Thames; but it appears to have acquired a bad reputation at a very early date—not for its own inherent qualities, but because the population which had gathered about this important neighbourhood converted what was once a clear stream into a dirty channel, by which the refuse and garbage of the houses might be carried to the Thames. Even as early as 1290 we find the White Friars, near the Temple, and the Black Friars, who were nearer to Ludgate Hill, complaining that the evil odours of the Fleet were so noisome as to prevail over the smell of the incense. This led to a cleansing and scouring and deepening of the river (a process which had to be repeated on many succeeding occasions), and thus in the reign of the Second Edward this swift little stream had become indeed the Fleet river, able to carry " ten or twelve ships' navies at once, with merchandise," that " were wont to come to the aforesaid Bridge of Fleet." Of course these ships were little more than canal boats of small draught; but the " river " was of some importance, for after leaving its source at Hampstead Hills it was fed by numerous wells—Clerk's Well, Skinner's Well, Fags' Well, Tode Well, and other wells at the North of London— from which it was surnamed the River of Wells. The tide flowed from the Thames, where now is Bridge Street, Ludgate Circus, and Farringdon Street, past the prison of the Fleet, and to the foot of *Holborn* Hill, where it united with the *Old Bourne*. Here it was afterwards crossed by one of four stone bridges—the principal of which was Fleet Bridge, uniting Ludgate Hill with Fleet Street, and, as Stow informs us, made or repaired at the charges of John Wells, Mayor of London in the year 1431. This doubtless replaced an earlier bridge of timber; and Fleet Bridge, with the other two bridges, one at Bridewell, the other at Fleet Lane, provided for the traffic of this main approach to London from the West, at the time that it was the centre of the Royal Court, and the trysting-place for the nobility. But all efforts to keep the Fleet River clean were ineffectual, and it eventually became known as the Fleet Ditch. The river had ceased to take sufficient water from its various feeders to keep the channel clear, the increased number of dwellings had diverted the water of the wells from their former course, and it became little else than a stagnant creek of the Thames, a receptacle for the filth and garbage of the neighbourhood.

The attempted restoration was unsuccessful, but the excavations brought to light some interesting relics in the shape of Roman pottery, and, deeper still, Roman coins and silver ring money. At Holborn Bridge were found two brazen Lares, about four inches long (a Bacchus and a Ceres), and a number of Saxon ornaments, seals, spurs, and weapons, and several later medals, crosses and crucifixes.

But we must give Time the slip again, and, recalling the period of the babbling and crystal stream, look across its channel to that further corner there by the back of Sir Polydore de Keyser's hotel, where stood the castle,—palace, —prison, the remnant of which has been known to living memory as the place of punishment for idle apprentices and sturdy vagabonds who now haunt the casual wards of the more attractive workhouses.

Bridewell.

As we have seen, the Old Wall encircling the City may be said to have commenced at the Tower and to have completed the circuit at about the foot of the present Blackfriars Bridge, on the Ludgate Hill side of the Fleet River. At the corner of the wall at this spot was a fortress, the remains of which, when it was pulled down, at a very early date, were used in building a palace named Bridewell, after the Well of St. Bridget close by. Bridewell, like the rest of the buildings of that magnitude, was both palace and fortress. It stood, and the last remains of it are hardly yet cleared away, just on the other side of the Fleet River, which brawled past its walls, and formed a kind of moat, giving access to the building by a water-gate. A frowning, bodeful pile enough it would seem to modern eyes—vast, yet lowering, full of bravery, show and rude luxury, but with a menacing look outward towards the common people. A stronghold like that of Mountfiquit on the Thames bank, south of the hill of Ludgate, and Baynard's Castle, further still, between Paul's Wharf and Puddle Dock, at the bottom of what is now known as St. Andrew's Hill, in the district of the "Royal Wardrobe," about which we will inquire presently. All three of these places—Bridewell, Mountfiquit, or Montfichet, and Baynard's Castle—represented Norman domination in the time of the Conqueror William, whose realm was built, like his castles, out of the material taken from both Roman and Saxon memorials. The barons who came in his train were quick in asserting their claims, and among them were Montfichet and Baynard, the first, probably proud enough to defy even William of Normandy, losing his place and local habitation, the second holding the castle named after him, and standing nearer to the broad stream of Thames, until after the reign of John, when the Baynards had forfeited their possession, and the castle had been conferred on the Fitzwalters, descendants of the Earls of Clare, and hereditary standard-bearers to the City of London.

Bridewell continued to be a royal palace till the death of Henry VIII., and it was here that he lodged (having had a way made connecting the building with the Black Friars) when the Pope's Legate and the proud Wolsey sat at the shameful trial of Queen Catharine. It is little to be wondered at, therefore, that the daughter of Catherine should shun the place, or that by the time that Edward VI. came to the throne it was deserted and fast going to decay. It was to Bishop Ridley that the benevolent scheme for converting it into a refuge for the houseless is to be attributed, and his curious but suggestive letter to the Secretary of State (Cecil, afterwards Lord Burleigh) is worth notice, "Good Mr. Cecil, I must be a suitor to you in our good Master Christ's cause. I beseech you to be good to Him. The matter is, sir, alas! He hath lain too long abroad (as you do know) without lodging, in the streets of London, both hungry, naked, and cold. Now, thanks be to Almighty God, the citizens are willing to refresh Him, and to give Him meat, drink, clothing, and firing; but, alas! sir, they lack lodging for Him. For in some one house, I dare say, they are fain to lodge three families under one roof. Sir, there is a large, wide, empty house of the King's Majesty's called Bridewell, that would wonderfully well serve to lodge Christ in, if He might find such good friends in the Court to procure in His cause. Surely I have such a good opinion of the King's Majesty, that if Christ had such faithful and hearty friends, who would heartily speak for Him, He should undoubtedly speed at the King's Majesty's hands. Sir, I have promised my brethren, the citizens, to move you, because I do take you for one that feareth God, and would that Christ should lie no more in the streets."

There is something nobly simple about this direct practical interpretation of the declaration " I was sick, and in prison, and ye visited me," and the man who wrote that letter was of the stuff of which martyrs are made.

And Cecil was not slow to back up the representations of the Bishop. Soon after (in 1553) the Lord Mayor and Commons of the City were called to Whitehall, and Bridewell was made over to them for an asylum and place of employment for the poor and destitute. But " Bridewell " included a prison as well as a refuge. Here, as at the Fleet, the Nonconformists, who were called Separatists, were held in durance, and suffered great privations, though they belonged to a body which was loyal and had no political significance. Here, too, the members of that body who were called Brownists formed what may be designated as the first Nonconformist Church—a church within their prison walls, whence, after long incarceration, they were taken to execution. Not till a later period did Bridewell become a " penitentiary " (?), a place of punishment intended for the reformation of the vicious, with special departments for idle and disobedient apprentices, and for women of bad reputation, of whom one of the last incarcerated there before the Great Fire destroyed the old building was one Madam Creswell, notorious even in those days of licence. Her name has survived chiefly because at her death, which took place in the gaol, it was found that she had expressed in her will a desire to have a sermon preached at her funeral, for which the preacher was to have ten pounds, but upon the condition that he was to say nothing but what was well of her. A preacher was with some difficulty found who undertook the task. He, after a sermon on the general subject of mortality and the good uses to be made of it, concluded by saying, " By the will of the deceased it is expected that I should mention her, and say nothing but what is *well* of her. All that I shall say of her, therefore, is this: she was born *well*, she lived *well*, and she died *well*. For she was born with the name Creswell, she lived in Clerkenwell, and she died in Brideswell."

Baynard's Castle.

The story of Baynard's Castle, and all the activities, intrigues, and conspiracies that were associated with it, forms a large section of the History of England, with which Ludgate Hill has always been prominently identified. When the long, narrow-windowed, frowning pile went out of the family of Bainardus—for what reason who can tell? except that the baron may have been another of the haughty knights who dared to quarrel with his liege, "the Bastard" —it went to the Fitzwalters, who were also Lords of Dunmow. Robert Fitzwalter, with his great retinue armed and in flaming surcoats, presented himself periodically at Ludgate, there to receive from the Mayor and citizens the great banner of London, which he was entitled to bear to the wars, if war there should be, or even the threat of it. He was a proud and puissant knight; but the story of his family is a tragic one. His daughter Matilda, one of the most beautiful maidens in England, attracted the base attentions of the false and licentious King John, who perhaps met her at some high festival in Baynard's Castle. It was in accordance with the monarch's detestable character that he should urge a dishonourable suit, which was resented indignantly both by the father and the daughter; but John was at once a fury and a sneak. He waited, and nursed his revenge and plotted, until he was able to drive Fitzwalter to take refuge in France. The daughter, then at his mercy, was taken away, and, it is said, died from poison—murdered by her royal suitor, whose passion had turned to hate. It is added, on the authority of an old chronicler, that her body was buried between the two pillars in the church at Dunmow, in Essex. Baynard's Castle was to have been demolished to complete the King's revenge, but the war with France followed quickly, and in the next year the encamped armies of the English and French kings lay opposite each other, during a truce, one on either side of a river. Tired of awaiting the signal for battle, an English knight challenged any one of the opposing force to break a lance with him. No sooner said than done. An unattended knight from the French camp came across the river, and having quickly reached the bank, at once mounted a horse, rode at the challenger, and with one tremendous blow of his lance, which was splintered to pieces with the shock, hurled both the antagonist and his horse to the ground. With one of his usual feeble profane oaths, John, who knew what prowess meant, and, in spite of his villainy was himself no mean adept in the art of war, cried out, "He were a king indeed who had such a knight." These words were heard by the bystanders, who had recognised in the successful warrior the renowned Fitzwalter, to whom they were duly reported, and on the following day he returned to the English camp, where he again sought the favour of the Sovereign who had so bitterly wronged him, and was graciously received, his possessions, and Baynard's Castle among them, being restored to the family. This is the story, and it has even been hinted that the challenge of the English knight, the response of Fitzwalter, the defeat, the restoration to favour, and all the rest of it, was a planned thing among Fitzwalter's friends, in order to get the doughty champion back again. Only on these grounds, and with the knowledge of what followed, can we consent to receive what is after all a rather vague narrative. The King could not restore the daughter of the man whom he had wronged, and there is something revolting in the idea of the father kneeling at the murderer's feet for the sake of regaining royal favour and worldly wealth. The tale does not correspond either with what we know of Robert Fitzwalter, who was at the head of the barons whose demands obtained from John the Great Charter at Runnymede. It was he who headed the knights when they went (probably from Baynard's Castle) to the King at the Temple to insist on the concessions, and in the appeal to arms which forced John to yield, Fitzwalter was chief of the barons, commander of their forces, "Marshal of the Army of God and of Holy Church."

One of the first things they did when they came from Bedford was to enter the City by Aldgate, and then to begin to plunder the houses of the Royalists and the Jews (who were usually mulcted on both sides), even taking the stones and materials of their dwellings to repair the City wall, which it was necessary to strengthen in case of siege. In

1586, two years before the Spanish Armada, and when Ludgate Hill was entirely rebuilt, there was found embedded among the stones of the ancient structure one bearing in Hebrew characters the words, "This is the ward (or home) of Rabbi Moses, the son of the honorable Rabbi Isaac."

In 1428 Baynard's Castle shared the fate which so often befell the more important as well as the meaner buildings of a city composed so largely of houses constructed of timber. It was almost entirely destroyed by fire. Having been afterwards granted to Humphrey Plantagenet, Duke of Gloucester, he rebuilt it, but on his attainder it again became Crown property, and by Henry VI. was granted to the Duke of York, who made it the scene of his ambitious plotting to secure the throne, and gathered above 1,000 armed men within its walls. After he was slain at the Battle of Wakefield the castle became the residence of his son Edward, his widow Cicely going to live in a mansion close by, near Paul's Wharf.

It is in the garden at Baynard's Castle that Shakespeare lays the scene between the Duke of York and the Earls of Salisbury and Warwick, in the play of *King Henry VI.*:—

> *York:* Now, my good lords of Salisbury and Warwick,
> Our simple supper ended, give me leave,
> In this close walk to satisfy myself,
> In craving your opinion of my title,
> Which is infallible, to England's crown.
>
> *   *   *   *   *
>
> *Warwick:* What plain proceeding is more plain than this?
> Henry doth claim the crown from John of Gaunt,
> The fourth son; York claims it from the third.
> Till Lionel's issue fails, his should not reign:
> It fails not yet, but flourishes in thee
> And in thy sons, fair slips of such a stock.
> Then, father Salisbury, kneel we together;
> And in this private plot be we the first
> That shall salute our rightful sovereign
> With honour of his birthright to the crown.

In the gloomy but stately pile of Baynard's Castle, which, with Crosby Hall, was then the most important of the City palaces, the treacherous Richard waited for the ripening of the plot that brought him to the throne. Here he held counsel with the Duke of Buckingham and the other creatures whom he used and crushed. After the proclamation at Paul's Cross, and the address from which the reverend preacher never recovered, but of the shame of which he pined and died, it was at Baynard's Castle that the wily usurper received his emissaries, and, as Shakespeare represents it, kept up a show of reluctance and of humility which was so subtly acted that we might almost imagine he had deceived himself and his instruments as well as the people. In the gallery of the great room—on each side of him a bishop—stands the crouching, sinister figure of the false Gloucester, and in subdued, pensive tone says, in mock rejection of the offered crown:—

> "Alas! why would you heap these cares on me?
> I am unfit for state and majesty:
> I do beseech you take it not amiss;
> I cannot nor I will not yield to you."

We know the end of the story, and may read how it was in the "high chamber" next the chapel that Richard had the Great Seal delivered to him on the day of his coronation; but retribution soon followed, and the Tudor was the next tenant of the grand old pile, to which he took such a liking that in 1501 he almost entirely rebuilt it. Doubtless its situation was pleasant. Its position on the river bank, when the Thames was the great highway from Greenwich to Westminster, and its secluded, beautiful, and spacious gardens, courtyards, and tilting-grounds made it a stately residence, though it was then prison-like and forbidding in the front that looked on the Thames. Henry VII., with great taste, made it, "not embattled, nor so strongly fortified, castle-like, but far more beautiful and commodious, for the entertainment of any prince of great estate, such as Philip of Austria, or the ambassadors from the King of the Romans, who were received here when they visited this country."

It was by water from Baynard's Castle that Prince Henry of Greenwich, afterwards Henry VIII., and his bride, Catherine of Aragon, were conducted in a splendid procession to the royal palace at Westminster, when the Mayor and commonalty of London, in barges garnished with standards, streamers, and pennons of their device, gave them their attendance; and there in the palace were such martial feats, such valiant jousts, such vigorous tourneys, such fierce fights at the barriers, as before that time was of no man had in remembrance.

But Baynard's Castle went finally out of the royal possession in the reign of Edward VI., when it became the residence of Sir William Sydney, the Royal Chamberlain, and from his hands passed to William Herbert, first Earl of Pembroke, who lived there in almost regal magnificence with his Countess Anne, sister of Queen Catherine Parr. At Edward's death the earl, who was a cautious nobleman, was induced to sign the famous document in favour of the claims of Lady Jane Grey, but backed out when he saw the danger, and was particularly practical in helping to proclaim Queen Mary, whose supporters met at Baynard's Castle. Thenceforward his caution seems not to have forsaken him, for he became a prominent personage in all the Court pageants, was appointed to receive Philip of Spain on his arrival, was present at the royal marriage at Winchester in 1564, and three months afterwards came up to London to the first Parliament under the newly-married sovereigns to his mansion of Baynard's Castle, followed by a retinue of two thousand horsemen in velvet coats with three laces of gold and gold chains, besides sixty gentlemen in blue coats, with his badge of the green dragon. Again we see him at the coronation of Queen Elizabeth, who appointed him Master of the Horse, and (he certainly was a careful man) accepted an invitation to supper at the grand old mansion by Ludgate Hill. At ten o'clock at night (a late hour for those times), after a sumptuous entertainment, he handed the Queen into her state barge at the water-gate of Baynard's Castle to the sound of music, and amidst the blaze of a grand display of fireworks, and thus attended her to Whitehall, surrounded by a flotilla of boats, and cheered by the acclamations of the citizens. These were rare times for Ludgate Hill, and Baynard's Castle was then in its palmy days. The earl was succeeded by his son Henry, whose countess was the

"Sidney's sister, Pembroke's mother" of Ben Jonson's verse.

The name of Baynard's Castle now only remains in that of the ward which is called Castle Baynard, unless we accept the curious allegation that in its early history a tract of well-watered land, or land furnished with springs, beyond Paddington, belonged to the founders of the family, and was known as Baynard's Water, now corrupted into Bayswater.

Paul's Wharf and Puddle Dock.

Next to Paul's Wharf, and still in the ward of Castle Baynard, is the ancient Puddle Dock, once a water-gate and wharf, named either after its owner or because it was a watering-place for horses, and so became trampled and puddled. There are allusions to it in the later days of Elizabeth, and no wonder, for it was close to the theatre at Blackfriars, where Shakespeare and Ben Jonson met, and of which we shall have to speak presently. In Jonson's "Bartholomew Fair" we read of Puddle Wharf,—

> "Which place we'll make bold with to call it our Abydos,
> As the Bankside is our Sestos."

And in "Hudibras" it is spoken of as though persons arrested for debt were sent there on their way to prison— perhaps either to Newgate, Bridewell, the Giltspur Street Compter, or the Fleet. Shadwell, too, in his "Epsom Wells" (1676), makes Clodpole say, "Is not this better than anything in that stinking town?" To which Lucia retorts, "Stinking town! I had rather be Countess of Puddle Dock than Queen of Sussex." More interesting still is the reference to the place in Shakespeare's will, in which he bequeaths to his daughter, Susannah Hall, his house in the Blackfriars "abutting upon a streete leading down to Puddle Wharffe, on the east part, right against the King's Majesty's Wardrobe . . . and now, or late, in the tenure or occupation of one William Ireland, or of his assignee or assignees." This description is in the conveyance, but the will says, "I gyve, will, bequeath, and devise unto my daughter, Susannah Hall . . . all that messuage or tenement, with the appurtenances, wherein one John Robinson dwelleth, scituat, lying, and being in the Blackfriars, in London, near the Wardrobe." The street leading down to Puddle Wharf is the present St. Andrew's Hill, so called from the Church of St. Andrew in the Wardrobe, but the old name was Puddle Dock Hill. It was in 1612 that Shakespeare bought the house in the place afterwards called, from its proprietor, Ireland Yard, and part of the house was built over a great gate leading to a building occupied by Henry, Duke of Northumberland.

Close to both Baynard's Castle and Puddle Dock was the harbour for corn coming from the Cinque Ports, and for centuries the successful rival of Billingsgate as a landing-place for fish and other commodities. It is said to have taken its name of Queenhithe, or *Ripa Regina* (Queen's bank or harbour), from the fact of its having become royal property, and the dues having been apportioned by King John to his mother, the queen of Henry II., from whom it descended to succeeding queens as belonging to them specially. But here we seem to have an example of one of those peculiar involutions of title which are a frequent puzzle to antiquaries and etymologists. There can be no doubt that in very early times the place was called Cornhithe, and Stow surmises that Queenhithe may have been a corruption of Cornhithe. If so, the royal proprietor may have taken advantage of the corruption, and confirmed it in order to fix the association between the place and its owner. But there is another possible derivation which the archæologists seem to have overlooked. It is possible that the place was originally named Quernehithe—querne being Saxon for a hand-mill, and afterwards probably for a corn-mill, so that we find querne and corn used indifferently. On the other side of St. Paul's, beyond Bowyer Row (Ludgate Hill) and along Ave Mary Lane by Paul's Gate in West Cheape, was the corn market, next to the shambles, and here—in the spot which would be the extreme end of Paternoster Row—was the church of St. Michael le Querne, or St. Michael ad Bladum (at the corne), destroyed in the Great Fire, and never rebuilt. It seems likely that near the corn harbour there may in early times have been a flour-mill, and that Querne-hithe may have been easily turned into

Queenhithe. The church of St. Michael, Queenhithe, in Upper Thames Street, with its vane in the form of a ship large enough to hold a bushel of grain, was built by Sir Christopher Wren immediately after the Fire of London, and contains some very finely carved woodwork on the doorway next the pulpit.

THE "WARDROBE."—PRINTING-HOUSE SQUARE.

The Wardrobe, to which Shakespeare refers, is close by (in our imagination), and if our fancy is not strong enough to picture it, we may find the place where it once stood, which has since retained the name of Wardrobe Court. There are so many quaint, shadowy nooks and corners still remaining in the whole of this ancient precinct of Doctors' Commons (it was not named Doctors' Commons till the time of Elizabeth, however), that a contemplative wayfarer with a little of the romantic lore of history might linger there for a long summer's day. The Wardrobe, which gave a second name to the Church of St. Andrew Wardrobe, was originally a mansion built by Sir John Beauchamp (son of the famous Guy, Earl of Warwick), after whose death, in 1359, it was sold to Edward III., and became, as its name implies, the depository for the Royal clothes, and a very extensive and valuable assortment of "toggery" some of our ancient monarchs must have had; as may be still seen by reference to the private accounts kept by the stewards at a time when the household expenses—the candles (which were a great item), the various rations of minstrels, pages, and attendants, the dishes for the Royal table, and the small beer of the servants' hall—were solemnly set forth and chronicled. Edward IV., who was as luxurious and self-indulgent as he was merciless, took care to have the Wardrobe well stocked with garments to set off his lanky but not ungraceful person on great state occasions, when it is, of course, a duty for a monarch to show his clothes. A manuscript account-book in the Harleian Collection shows that from April to Michaelmas, 1481, the sum of £1174 5s. 2d. was received by the Wardrobe-keeper, most of which was spent on velvet at 8s. to 16s. a yard; silks from Montpellier, "velvet upon velvet," and "black cloths of gold," at

40*s*. a yard; satins at 6*s*. to 12*s*.; camlets 30*s*. a-piece; sarcenets, 4*s*. to 4*s*. 2*d*.; damask, 8*s*. Surely the Queen must have had her wardrobe here, too; and we have only to remember the relative value of money in those days, when the carcass of an ox could be bought for five-and-twenty shillings, and a sheep for about three, to compute how luxuriously the Court dressed, and what fine birds were made of such fine feathers. Feather beds, with bolsters, for the King, cost 16*s*. 8*d*. each; a pair of double-soled Spanish shoes (they were long in the toes then), unlined, cost 1*s*. 4*d*.; a pair of black leather boots 6*s*. 8*d*.; hats 1*s*.; and ostrich feathers 10*s*. a-piece. Sometimes the King lodged at the Wardrobe, perhaps while Baynard's Castle was being cleaned down, and then there was a washing bill. Of course, we must take the wardrobe to be that of the royal household, and the cost will not be so extravagant, especially as other items were charged in the amount; for instance, that of book-binding—for we find an entry of 20*s*. paid to Piers Baudwyn (Peter Baldwin he would be now), stationer, "for binding, gilding, and dressing of a book called 'Titus Livius,' and 16*s*. each for a Bible, a 'Froissard,' 'Josephus,'" and other books.

This would seem to imply that stationers had already settled in the locality which they have occupied ever since—near Ludgate Hill and St. Paul's; and we must remember that at that date (1481) copper-plate printing had been invented in Germany thirty years before, and that Caxton had been five years at the Almonry at Westminster with his press for printing books with movable types. The lever that was to move the world and change the face of society had already been applied. And here close by is the place that may be called the representative core and centre of that great power of the press which followed in due course. The King's Printers, whose House, which formerly stood in Printing-House Square, and gave it its name, are no longer there; nor does the house itself exist. John Bill, who printed the Royal proclamations of Charles II., and the first *London Gazette*, established in that reign, had no successor in the Square. The last of the King's printers who had their house here were Charles Eyre and William

Strahan; and in 1770 the King's Printing-house was removed to New Street, Gough Square, where George Eyre and Andrew Strahan succeeded to it. Of the great business of Eyre and Spottiswoode, which is still in the neighbourhood, and near to Ludgate Hill, all the world knows.

But before the King's Printing-house had been removed, a vast power had appeared in Printing-House Square. On the 1st of January, 1788, the first number of the *Times* was issued from the printing-office that had there been set up by Mr. Walter. In 1803 the *Times* became the most important newspaper in the world; for many years exercised a power which was recognised, and was sometimes feared, all over Europe, and was the precursor of the enormous influence of the newspaper press at the present time. After the Great Fire the " Royal Wardrobe " was removed to the Savoy, and afterwards to Buckingham Street. The last Master was Ralph, Duke of Montague; and it was abolished in 1709.

Round Old St. Paul's.

But returning to the now half-demolished but traditional neighbourhood, just beyond Ludgate towards St. Paul's, we come again to Paul's Wharf, which old Stow describes as "a large landing-place with a common stair upon the River Thames, at the end of a street called Paul's Wharf Hill, which runneth down from Paul's Chain." Here within a great gate once stood a number of houses said to have been called in the leases granted by the Dean and Chapter the Camera Dianæ, or Diana's Chamber. The legendary reasons for this name being given to the place, as stated by Maitland, are curious and highly improbable, viz., that there existed there a spacious building in the form of a labyrinth, which had been constructed there by Henry II. for the concealment of the fair Rosamond Clifford, and that there was a subterranean passage from the place to Baynard's Castle. Maitland declares that for a long time there remained some evidence of tedious turnings and windings—and that is exceedingly probable—for within living memory some of the adjacent courts and alleys were mazy enough; but why Rosamond Clifford should have been called Diana, or why there should have been a labyrinth close to St. Paul's to imitate that at Woodstock, when the place was full of prying eyes and bustling activity, is not easily explained. Probably there may have been some building used by the ecclesiastics, and even called the Diana Chamber, as has been ingeniously suggested, from the designs of some old tapestry on the walls, or even from a tradition of the Temple of Diana that was supposed to have been on the site of the Cathedral. For we are now amidst the dependencies of St. Paul's—here in Paul's Chain—so called from the chain or barrier drawn across the roadway to prevent traffic during the time of Divine Service, the barrier on the north side being a wooden beam. It was at Paul's Chain that the famous arithmetician and caligraphist Edward Cocker lived in 1660, where he taught the arts which he professed "in an extraordinary manner at his dwelling on the south side of St. Paul's Church," and it was here that he wrote "The Pen's Ascendancy," a remarkable illustration of his skill, but one by which his name was less remembered than by his arithmetical accuracy, which has even come down to us traditionally in the phrase "according to Cocker." In Godliman Street, Paul's Chain, was Paul's Bakehouse, which has left its name to the court on which it stood. Here the bread for the church and its clergy was baked, and at Paul's Brewhouse, at the corner of the entrance to Doctors' Commons from the Churchyard, the beer was supplied to those Churchmen who, like Bishop Still, loved ale whether new or old. St. Paul's Coffee House stood on the site of he brewery, and that was followed by the Paul's Head Tavern, and afterwards, as Sam Weller says in the inimitable adventures of Mr. Pickwick, "Bookseller's at one corner, hot-el on the other, and porters in the middle as touts for licenses."

But we must abandon all notions of the present aspect of St. Paul's and the Churchyard if we desire to picture to ourselves the Cathedral—not that of Ethelbert, but its successor. The old Saxon church, of which Melitus was first bishop and Erkenwald the fourth, was entirely destroyed by fire, so William the Conqueror began to construct a vast pile upon the site in 1083; and it was again injured by fire in 1137, before it was really finished—for the building

Church of St. Gregory

OLD ST. PAUL'S.

was not completed till the reign of Henry III. It took nearly two centuries to complete such a stupendous work in days when kings so often wanted sudden "benevolences" of money, that even the Church had to wait. Old St. Paul's was an enormous building—inelegant, and without the grander and purer lines and beautiful ornamentation which distinguish the Gothic architecture of other cathedrals, but vast and imposing; and with an interior which was regarded as one of the finest sights in the world, because of its great size, its many gorgeous shrines, and the numerous multitude of priests and acolytes who officiated at the altar, the chapels, the chantries, and the choir.

To begin with, the old Cathedral did not stand in the same direction as the present one. The west front of the ancient structure came much further towards Ludgate, and the building stood, as it were, more square with the two main thoroughfares of Chepe and Ludgate Hill. It covered a much greater space, for its extent was so enormous that that alone was sufficient to make any pile of building imposing. The entire edifice measured 690 feet in length by 130 in breadth, and above the great height of the spacious roof rose a timber spire to a height of 520 feet, surmounted not only by a ball and cross, but by a large gilt eagle, which served as a weathercock. The wall which bounded the churchyard ran along by the present streets of Ave Maria Lane, Paternoster Row, Old Change, Carter Lane, and Creed Lane, and in this ample, partly-enclosed area were included many buildings and many appendages to the church, the most historically important of which was Paul's Cross—a structure the antiquity of which is not to be determined by any record. It stood on the north side, at a spot now marked, within the present garden of the Cathedral. It was at Paul's Cross that the citizens assembled for the folkmote or for any public purpose—either political, social, or ecclesiastical; and afterwards proclamations, State sermons, denunciations, declarations of allegiance, or even the trial and condemnation of public offenders, were constantly associated with this famous landmark of Old London.

The early history of the old Cathedral was one of continual architectural restoration, and the growth of artistic taste which had been developed in the reign of the Third Henry was nowhere more practically exemplified than at St. Paul's, under that energetic Churchman and skilful designer Bishop Roger, who was surnamed Niger. A new steeple was completed in 1221, and a new choir in 1240, and the Bishop depended not directly upon King, Pope, or Prelate, but indirectly upon the people, and very artfully he went to work. He induced nearly all his brother bishops in England to issue letters to their clergy granting "indulgences" for a certain number of days to all those persons who, having penance to perform and being penitent, should assist in the building. Such was the alacrity with which these appeals were answered, that St. Paul's, the tiny Church of St. Gregory, standing as it were in the arms of the mother church at the south-west corner, and the subterranean Church of St. Faith, which occupied the space beneath the crypt, were soon completed, and pictures, shrines, vestments, and sacred vessels and ornaments for the high altar, all richly dight with gold, silver, and precious stones, were among the costly presents that told of the general interest in making the great Cathedral worthy of its position in the very centre of the English metropolis. Charles Knight, in his "London," has called up a picture of Old St. Paul's in the beginning of the 15th century which is exceedingly graphic.

We are to imagine ourselves now passing up the hill. Behind us lies the moderately broad and rapid Fleet River, with its numerous vessels riding quietly at anchor. We pass through Lud Gate, and so to the entrance into the Cathedral enclosure. The place is crowded with people, chiefly of the poorer classes, who are being fed by the ecclesiastical officers. It is evidently a day of high festival, no less, indeed, than the festival of the conversion of the patron saint—St. Paul. Before we pass through the sumptuous western gates of the church let us cast a glance at the Bishop's palace where London House Yard since stands. Here it was that Edward III. and his queen were lodged after the great tournament in Smithfield, when so many goodly knights appeared, the charger of each knight led by a beautiful dame mounted on a palfrey, and, as Froissart tells us, "there was goodly dancing in the Queen's lodging in the presence of the King and his uncles and ladies and damoiselles till it was day, which was time for every person to draw to their lodgings, except the King and Queen, who lay there in the Bishop's palace." But we must pass on to the Cathedral before the great business of the day begins. We enter, and are at once fixed in amazement at the scene of enchantment suddenly visible. An apparently endless perspective of lofty arches lost in the distance in a luminous mist—a confused blaze of many-coloured streams of light, a great number of persons in all kinds of dresses moving to and fro, sublime sounds, at once press upon and bewilder the attention. As we gaze more steadily the wonderful perspective becomes gradually clear, until at last, for nearly *seven hundred feet*, we can follow the range—unbroken from the tesselated marble pavement below to the roof with its gilded groins above—of arches upon arches, and of the dim but richly-coloured painted windows at the top. The only, and that very slight, interruption is the low screen which crosses the pavement far down, probably about the centre of the pile. The glorious vista is terminated by a rose window of great size, but appearing from hence scarcely larger than the flower from which it borrows its name, whilst its colours, while revelling in the intensest of dyes, appear mingled into one glowing but nameless hue. As the eye wanders from this, the first impressive feature of the place, it falls upon the huge lighted tapers on the different altars that we see scattered about the nave and aisles, then to the kneeling people before them—here a large group, there a solitary individual.

As we pace along the nave, and the transepts open on either hand, magnificent shrines lining the walls, tall crosses with tapers before them, and gorgeous pictures, are seen at every step. There seems no end to the wealth that has been lavished upon the place. Gold, silver, rubies, emeralds, pearls begin even to lose their value from their profusion. A kind of low, confused hum pervades the church, above which may be continually distinguished the voices of the priests, who are performing the duties of their respective chantries, scattered along the entire length of the nave, aisles, and transepts—seventy or eighty in number; whilst grandly towering over all we hear the chant and responses of the choral multitude. The Cathedral is now rapidly becoming full. Noblemen, warriors, citizens, and labourers, arrayed in all kinds of materials—satin, damask, cloth of gold and silver, and the plain but good old English broadcloth of different colours—their dresses exhibiting every variety of fashion, as little hoods, long gowns, short coats, long piked shoes, parti-coloured hose, and ornamented, in so many cases, with gems and embroidery, that, as Knighton observes, "it is impossible to distinguish the rich from the poor, the high from the low." Nor are the ladies generally less fantastically or less sumptuously arrayed. The preparations for the coming festivity are now begun. Noiseless figures are gliding to and fro, setting up additional tapers in every part of the church where there is room and convenience for placing them; but a short time elapses, and hundreds of such lights are burning in every direction. Hark! the sound of horns blown more loudly than skilfully reverberates through the pile; and, as if it were some wizard's signal, there is a general cessation of the devotional business of the place. The devotee starts from his knees, the penitent sinner wipes the tears from his cheeks, the grave become gay, the gloomy look cheerful, as all eagerly press forward and line the intercommunications of the nave; first in a single row, then a second behind that, then a third, till both aisles are filled, and little more than a lane is left for the passage of the coming procession down the central part of the nave. The officers with their gilded staves have to bestir themselves even to keep that clear. Again and again blow the horns, the western doors are thrown back, and a strange procession enters, consisting of a group of horn-blowers, then a body of ruddy-cheeked yeomen and others, bearing, on a kind of frame raised aloft, the doe, which the family of Baud are bound yearly to offer in procession at the high altar on this day, in addition to a buck on the summer feast called the Commemoration of St. Paul, both being in lieu of certain lands granted to Sir William Baud, in the third year of Edward I., by the Church, to be enclosed within his park of Toringham, in Essex. Immediately before the doe-bearers marches proudly the keeper, or huntsman, clad in green coat and hood, and bearing beneath his belt a sheaf of peacock arrows, in his hand a bow, and, as Chaucer sings of one of his characters—

> "A nut head had he with a brown viságe,
> Of woodcraft could he well all the uságe."

On moves the procession towards the choir, which it enters, and so to the steps of the high altar at its extremity. There it is met by the Dean and Chapter, arrayed in rich copes and robes, jewelled and embroidered, and wearing garlands of roses on their heads. The head of the doe is now divided from the body, and, whilst the body is at once sent off to be baked, the head is fixed on a spear, and borne before the cross in the usual daily procession, which now starts towards the western door. This reached, the keeper makes the whole neighbourhood ring again with his lusty horn, and, before the sound has well died away, it is answered from different quarters of the City by similar instruments. All the parties are now dismissed with a small present in money to their dinners, provided by the Dean and Chapter, whilst the keeper will also have to receive his customary five shillings, and his loaf of bread stamped with the image of St. Paul.

So ends this portion of the business of the day; but the most splendid is yet to come—the commemoration of St. Erkenwald's burial in the Cathedral, where, we are told, his "glorious merits did shine forth miraculously." Again through the western door comes a procession winding from the Bishop's palace, this time the Bishop himself at its head, having the Dean on his right hand, other distinguished officers of the church on his left, and followed by nearly all the clergy of his diocese, with all the customary paraphernalia of the church processions during such high solemnities. The sumptuousness of their appearance beggars description. The Bishop wears a long, snow-white robe almost concealing his feet, above which is another of ruby-coloured silk, reaching a little below the knee, open at the sides, embroidered all over in the most exquisite manner with representations of animals, birds, and flowers, and having a deep border, which consists chiefly of rows of interlaced pearls. From the low, upright collar of this upper robe, down the centre of the front to the bottom, extends a band formed of one entire mass of precious stones, of different colours, and arranged in a variety of close patterns. The golden mitre on his head, the golden pastoral staff in his hand, are each similarly ornamented. Towards the shrine of St. Erkenwald slowly moves the procession amidst the fragrant perfumes shed around by incense-bearers from their silver censers, now up the nave, thence through one of the aisles, and so round to the shrine at the back of the high altar. This is the most gorgeous piece of combined architecture, sculpture, and decoration even in a Cathedral rich in such works. Rising from behind a kind of table covered with jewels and precious stones of all kinds, including small shrines, rings, and silver girdles, the gifts of the pious, appears a lofty pyramidal Gothic structure in the purest and most exquisitely decorated style; the outlines formed by pinnacles rising one above another towards a single pinnacle in the centre at the top, and the central portion consisting of three slender windows side by side, and an exceedingly elegant one filling the triangular space above. A railing encloses the whole for the preservation of the invaluable treasures lying on the table within, or that have been used in the adornment of the shrine. Among the former we may find the sapphire stone which Richard de Preston, citizen and grocer of London, gave to be placed here for the curing of infirmities in the eyes, appointing at the same time that proclamation should be made of its virtues. Solemn masses for the repose of the dead are now said; the indulgences granted to all who visit the shrine, and to those who bring oblations, are explained. The words fall upon no dull or unheeding ears; they come pressing around, rich and poor, lay and ecclesiastic, depositing their gifts of money or jewels or whatever else the tastes or means of the owners instigate, the very poorest having at least a taper for their favourite shrine.

All is still at last. Prelates, clergy, choristers have gone;

the lights, save those which burn perpetually before the different chantries, shrines, and altars are extinguished; the rich western window, lit up by a sudden burst of sunshine, seems to glow with preternatural radiance and splendour, and throws its warm light far along the pavement, and, catching the edge of the gilded crucifix raised aloft in the centre of the nave, makes it appear even more brilliant than the taper by its side.

There may be some other processions outside—of Franciscans, or those Dominicans who are hereafter to give the name to the precinct of Blackfriars; but a goodly number of visitors stay in the Cathedral to look round at the superb altar of Our Lady and Our Lady's chapel, the sculptured image of Our Lady with its lamp constantly burning, and an iron box at the foot of the statue for the offerings of the pious. Behind this statue, on the right of the nave as we approach the choir, is the low sculptured tomb of Sir John Beauchamp, with his effigy in complete armour lying on the top, and the lower part decorated with painted and sculptured shields. Not much farther, and we look up to the great height of the four arches that support the high tower of the Cathedral, and yet spring so lightly upward that they seem incapable of bearing the square tower that rises to 260 feet, and in its turn supports the spire of wood covered with lead, which is 274 feet more.

LUDGATE HILL AND PRISON.—LOLLARDS' TOWER.

Paternoster Row, Ave Maria Lane, Creed Lane—yes, the stationers have settled here—the stationers and text writers, sellers of prayers, rosaries, hornbooks, A B C's, and such volumes as those which Edward IV. had bound, "tooled," and gilded. Stationers' Hall is not yet founded, but here is the building which is to become the centre of that craft and mystery on which the progress of the world is so greatly to depend. Between Amen Corner and Bowyer Row (hereafter to be named Ludgate Street), stands a great house of stone and wood, the house of John, Duke of Bretagne, in the time of Edward II., and going down to the Earls of Pembroke, after whom it is named Pembroke Inn. It is worthy of note that these great mansions of the nobility in London are called inns, and that in the City and its Liberties—within the encircling wall—are a number of such goodly piles, with their courtyards and surrounding lodgings, where retainers and men-at-arms dwell and have their rations served to them. Close by, near Newgate Market and Prison, is Warwick Inn, in Eldenesse Lane (but soon to be called Warwick Lane), the great mansion of the Nevills, wherein "the King-maker" takes up his abode when Henry VI. has summoned the estates of the realm to London. Great doings are there then, for along Ludgate Hill march the Earl's men, six hundred of them, clad in red jackets, embroidered before and behind with the cognisance of the Nevills, that ragged staff which has rallied its bearers in many a hard-fought field. Away to Warwick House tramp they, amidst sharp ring of arms and the shouts of the people, and great state will be kept, for there will be often as many as six oxen eaten at a breakfast, and every tavern will be full of the Earl's meat, for he that has any acquaintance in that house may go there and take so much of sodden and roast meat as he can prick and carry away on a long dagger. Yes, there are brave doings in these days about that quarter, and in the large open space fronting St. Paul's and behind Ludgate. Once more will the people in Bowyer's Row do a brisk trade, and the clink of anvils and the sound of carpentry be heard. Still later, and in the great Smoothfield, by the Priory and Hospital of Saint Bartholomew, there will again be jousts and tournaments, and from the Tower, by the old Roman road of Watling Street, and so along Knightrider Street to the front of St. Paul's, will come the champions, the squires, the men-at-arms, to attend the Weapon Show, or, as the Scotch call it, the Wapin-schaw. There is a blare of trumpets, a crash and clatter of iron, a flash of gold and steel, quaint devices and gay colours of banner and pennon and painted shield, as the cavalcade rides by, with heralds in tabards ablaze with gold and crimson, pursuivants with jewelled housings and truncheons of office, ladies on ambling palfreys, or borne in litters, gently heaving forward, as they are carried by low, easy-paced horses, and surrounded with a glittering retinue of pages.

The prisons are full enough. Here at Ludgate itself the

cry of the poor debtors who are confined in the gaol where the gate joins the City wall is heard daily. It is a wretched place, and the abode of the wretched who are kept there by remorseless creditors. Merchants and tradesmen who have been ruined by losses at sea are among them; and it has had an evil reputation ever since the days of Richard II., when it was first used as a place of confinement, not for evil-doers, but for the unfortunate. But it has its romantic story; for here, according to the old chroniclers, was a prisoner, one Robert Forster, who, begging at the grate with the alms-box into which benevolent donors cast their money for the relief of the inmates, was asked by a wealthy widow what sum of money would pay his debts and set him free. He replied that twenty pounds would suffice (a good round sum in those days, for he had been a merchant of London); and she at once paid it, and took him into her service, where he behaved with such discretion that she afterwards married him, and he built up a still larger fortune, and became Lord Mayor of London. This worthy pair, remembering the sufferings of the poor debtors, enlarged the prison, added to it a chapel for the inmates, and provided that in future there should be free lodging and water, to which effect an inscription was placed outside the gate. That this was a real relief may be understood when we learn that at other prisons for debtors lodgings and even water had to be paid for; and but for the alms-box, the broken victuals from the Lord Mayor's table, and other contributions of the charitable, many of those who were kept in hopeless durance would have perished of want.

Even over the tiny church of St. Gregory, snuggling there in the very elbow of St. Paul's, is the Lollards' Tower, where heretics are tormented and martyrs have lived and died within the sound of the great Cathedral, and of the campanile that stands just beyond apart from the church—the bell-tower whence in older times came the peal that summoned citizens to the folkmote, and rang out the chime of rejoicing, or the alarum that gave warning of strife, and called men to arms. So, amidst the splendid shows, the gorgeous pageants, the solemn celebrations, the ever-changing and abundant vitality of this great thoroughfare from the hill foot to East

Chepe, are heard the undertones of misery and persecution, the wail against cruelty and oppression. Amidst the vigorous life one might almost turn to find some meaning of that symbolic "dance of death" which is painted on the walls of the cloister surrounding the Pardon Church Haugh, in the churchyard just beyond the bishop's house, to the east by Paternoster Row. The father of Thomas Becket built that chapel, and the strange, weird dance was added but lately (for we are now in the reign of Henry VI.), at the special request of Jenkin Carpenter, citizen and mercer. This dance of death is already a favourite delineation for cloister walls, and is an illustration of a poem written by one Machabre, a German, after whom it is sometimes called "the dance of Machabre." It is a "moral" performance, and consists of a long train of figures representing persons of all degrees and stations, from the Pope to the lowest beggar or outcast, who perform a procession or dance each with a skeleton partner, and heading the train the bony spectre who flourishes his emptying hour-glass. The grotesque memento may have its moral uses, but better for the true instruction of the people, if the people could only read, would be the "faire library with faire written books in vellum just placed in the room over the east side of the cloister by Walter Shyrington, Canon Residentiary of St. Paul's and Chancellor of the Duchy of Lancaster."

The "Bell Savage."—Its Origin.

But we must return to our standpoint beside the old Bell Savage Inn, for the history of that ancient building emerges in the reign of Henry VI., when one John French legally conveys " to his mother for her life all that tenement or inn, with its appurtenances, called Savage's Inn, otherwise called the Bell on the Hoop." This is the first regular mention of the inn; it was evidently in possession of the Savage family, and as there are indications that it became the property of one Isabella Savage, Stow thinks that it was from her that the old inn got its name. The title which it bore in more modern times—La Belle Sauvage—has probably one of two derivations. It was the custom of the wits, poets, and players, and indeed of almost everybody of the time of the Tudors and the Stuarts, to make anagrams, and sometimes to convert the anagrams into rebuses or pictorial tokens. We see such among many of the tradesmen's and tavern tokens still preserved, and it is therefore easy to suppose that Isabella Savage, or Bella Savage, might be converted into La bel Savage, or, in more modern French, La Belle Sauvage. The other possible origin of the sign, according to Pennant, is mentioned in the *Spectator* by Addison. "As for the Bell Savage," he says, "which is the sign of a savage man standing by a bell, I was formerly very much puzzled upon the cause of it, till I accidentally fell into the reading of an old romance translated out of the French, which gives an account of a very beautiful woman who was in a wilderness, and is called in the French La Belle Sauvage, and is everywhere translated by our countrymen the Bell Savage." With all grave reverence for Mr. Addison and Mr. Pennant, we can scarcely think the old French romance was known here before the Wars of the Roses, and the fact of the old place being called Savage's Inn, and having the token, as it were, of a bell, sufficiently accounts for the savage man and the bell, which was the rebus for Bell Savage. But let us reflect for a minute. The place is sometimes called the *Belly* Savage, and in later times the *Old* Bell Savage. This may suggest a rather simple derivation, when we consider that the ancient building, like the great pile which more than covers its area to-day, was close to, and one portion of it may have opened upon, the Ballium or Bailey (which at one time would have been crossed by a bail or bar of wood), the residence of the high bailiff, and the bail or boundary of the district. Now, as the inn was the mansion of the Savage family, and near the Bailey or Ballium, it is at least conceivable that it would come to be known as the Bail or Bailey Savage Inn, and afterwards the *Old* Bail or Bailey Savage Inn. The similarity in sound between bail and bell might have justified the pictorial token, and the derivation, at all events, seems probable. But, as we have before mentioned, the old place was not an inn for public entertainment in the times that we have been depicting. In its courtyards were tenements for retainers or tenants of the owners of the mansion, and its great gate shut it from the roar and turmoil of Ludgate Hill.

The Hill in Old Times.

We can scarcely picture to ourselves what the streets of London were like in those days—the houses, mostly of timber and wood, cement or plaster, built in overhanging storeys, evidently the best way of making each storey preserve from the effects of rains and storms that which was beneath it. Not till the time of Edward IV. do we hear of brick houses, and glass windows were by no means common till long afterwards. The middle of the streets began to be paved in Henry VIII.'s reign, and though there was then much magnificence and display, the customs were not over cleanly. The floors were commonly of clay, strewed with rushes, beneath which often lay unmolested, as Erasmus tells us, "an ancient collection of beer, grease, fragments of fish, etc., etc., and everything that is nasty."

Even the City was not lighted at night till the reign of Henry V., and then the illumination was with lanterns slung upon ropes or haybands which crossed the streets—an arrangement which might be applied to our electric lighting. The City Watch in the time of Henry VIII. had grown to be a stately body of men, and when they went out for their muster on the Eve of St. John the sight was one that the King himself liked to look upon; but robbery had been rife, and in the dark and devious bye-ways and alleys thieves and footpads had easily escaped. The cry, "Hang out your lights!" and the ordinance of the City that every householder should hang outside his dwelling a horn lantern and a whole candle somewhat mitigated the evil; but it was as difficult to enforce the law as it was to compel the extinction of fires when the bells rang the curfew (or *couvre feu*) to warn housekeepers and servants that at eight o'clock at night they must place upon the embers the metal lid or cover that should extinguish the burning wood or coal, and so prevent the danger of houses being suddenly found ablaze in a neighbourhood where there was wood and thatch to spread it, and but a poor supply of water—even though there were twelve great conduits, or leaden cisterns, in various parts of the City. The need for the *couvre feu* may very well be imagined if we remember that there were no chimneys; the hearth was in the middle of the room, the smoke escaping by *louvres* or flues either in walls or roof; "whence," as John Aubrey, the antiquarian, who lived in 1678, says, " comes the saying 'round about our coal fire.'" "Public Inns," he goes on to tell us, "were rare" (in the country he means). "Travellers were entertained at religious houses for three days together, if occasion served. The meetings of the gentry were not at taverns, but in the fields or forests, with hawks and hounds and their buglehorns, in silken baldricks."

Queen Elizabeth on Ludgate Hill.

But a great change has taken place in the manners as well as the customs of the people of London, although there may be only a small improvement in some of their dwellings, and in the multitude of conveniences which we are accustomed to regard as the signs of increased civilisation. The Priory of Bartholomew has been suppressed, the Black Friars unhoused and disestablished. For a time only Mary succeeded in undoing what her father did, or doing what her brother, the young Edward, undid; and now, with the Spaniard at bay and the Pope in check, the figure of Elizabeth comes to fill the great place that could have been filled by none else. A youthful, slight, but determined figure, with clear, intrepid eyes, which the grim shadow of the Tower has not dimmed; with her father's imperial temper, and the Boleyn art of winning the loyalty of brave and gifted men; with grand, noble impulses, and second thoughts of dissimulation; with courage unshrinking, and insight that seldom fails; with learning enough to talk with the wise, and accomplishments to please the gay, and compel a true admiration in the midst of sycophants—a Tudor, perhaps more like her grandfather, Henry VII., than her father, except in the early days when he was Henry of Greenwich. The bells are ringing out till every steeple rocks; flags are flying; balconies are hung with tapestry and velvet pile; at every conduit in the City some allegorical show is set; the streets are decked with flowers, and gay colours flaunt from every window. All Ludgate is astir; the shops and stalls are full of wares, and the City 'prentices, in their cloaks and caps, shout till they are too hoarse to cry, "What d'ye lack?" The taverns are full, and great piles of brawn and stacks of bread, flagons of ale and bottles of sack and canary, salads of colewort and mighty rounds of beef, capons, and a dozen kinds of meat and drink, of which the names are now almost forgotten, though the things themselves survive, are ready for the feasters, who will soon come in, hungry from much loyalty; for the shouting of a great crowd is heard coming from Chepe, and in its midst, seated in an open litter, seen of all the people, is the Princess Elizabeth, soon to be known as Good Queen Bess. It is as though a great pall had been lifted from the land, and there is a new light in men's faces, a new hope in their hearts; and only a few, dark and moody, slip aside as the trampling throng comes on, and get them away, wondering whether the times of Mary have really passed away, and her heretic sister will uphold the Reformation and defy the authority of Rome.

By-the-bye, it should be mentioned that among the draperies that hang from the beetling windows of the citizens' houses are rich *Turkey carpets*, for even in the days of the Eighth Harry ships trading to the East to Tripoli and Baruth brought these costly fabrics for the wealthy merchants and substantial citizens, who now dress as richly and furnish their rooms as sumptuously as the nobles themselves, with cloth of arras and silk adorning the walls, and silver plate upon their sideboards, where pike and sturgeon, peacock, venison pasty, chine of beef, ruffs and reeves, swan, heron, and capons, puddings, pies, and cream are piled for the feast—except between Michaelmas and Whitsuntide, when the meat, or the beef, at all events, is salted, and no cattle are slaughtered, even for the Royal table. The Turkey carpets, by-the-bye are not placed upon the floors, where rushes or matting still do duty, but are used to cover chairs and tables, or as drapery for wall and door. The outer appearance of many of the houses, even about Ludgate Hill, is poor and mean, but quaint and picturesque too,* and they are divided by larger mansions and imposing buildings. The streets are irregular, winding, and dirty; there are no coaches or carriages; but all along the banks of the Thames Strandwards, and at intervals from the Temple to the Tower, the palaces of the nobles have their gardens running down to the river, where, at wharves or landing-stages, the family barge and its attendant wherries are moored, for people who do not care to walk travel mostly on the silent highway, and the waterman's business flourishes. There are laws (made by Henry VIII.) stringently imposing heavy fines on those who pollute the Thames with any sort of refuse. Robert Brooke, Chaplain to Henry VIII., has long ago done much for supplying water to the City by the invention of making leaden pipes for conveying the water underground from Hampstead Heath, St. Marylebone, Hackney, Muswell Hill, and the springs of St. Agnes le Clair, Hoxton.

Surely, as Elizabeth passed here by the Bell Savage, and cast a glance at the spot where we are standing, she must have had a sudden sad memory (she is one who knows little of fear) of the mad expedition of Wyatt, which ended here so tragically, and for which, though she has affirmed she neither knew nor approved it, she was near finding a grave within the walls of the Tower, whence she has just come to be made Queen. Sir Thomas Wyatt was the son of the poet who had been so close a friend of the Earl of Surrey, and so faithful a partisan of Anne Boleyn. He was opposed to the marriage of Mary to the King of Spain, and raised an insurrection, which, if it had been successful, would probably have brought Elizabeth earlier to the throne—at a cost of civil war. So formidable was Wyatt's following that Mary had to go to the City, and there, at the Guildhall, disown any fixed intention to marry against the objections of the people. By this she gained the help of the citizens to put down the rebellion; but Wyatt had raised an army in Kent, and held Rochester, where he was joined by a number of Londoners, who had been sent against him as a part of the army of the Duke of Norfolk. Norfolk's army

* One or two houses of a rather later date are still standing in Fleet Street, and others in Holborn.

fled, and the rebels came on to Deptford, and thence to Southwark, but, being denied admission that way, went to Kingston rather than attack the City. The Queen was then at the Guildhall prevaricating, and had Wyatt not delayed because of a brokendown field-gun at Turnham Green, he might have gained London, for he forced back his opponents, restored the broken bridge at Kingston by a bridge of barges, and while some of his officers deserted him, and rode on to the City to entrap him, had come to Charing Cross, and repulsed a thousand men under Sir John Gage, who was obliged to retreat within Whitehall Palace, amidst the shrieks and cries of treason and general uproar of the Court, who expected nothing less than to be slaughtered outright. But Wyatt was away towards Ludgate, the Queen's troops and Pembroke's horse closing on his rear. He was too late. Lord William Howard was already there with the citizens, and the gate had become a fortress of armed men. He had thought he needed only to show himself, and that the citizens would welcome the enemy of that Spaniard who was coming to England to be their master; but he was undeceived when Howard shouted, "Avaunt, traitor! thou shalt not come in here." The troops filled the Strand, and cut off his retreat at Temple Bar. A fierce and deadly fight must soon make the Fleet run blood. Here, by the Old Bell Savage, is the bench on which he flung himself in despair of a cause already lost. He would strive to return, but it could only be by fighting, and the fighting, already begun, would be hopeless. Clarencieux, King at Arms, comes riding through the press, and begs that he will save the great bloodshed that must ensue, when, perchance, he himself may find the Queen merciful. It was the only course left, except to sacrifice a number of brave men to his own pride; and, surrendering to Sir Maurice Berkely, who called to him to leap up behind him on his horse, and so carried him through the ranks of the soldiers to Whitehall, Wyatt passed out of the streets, and to the Tower, whence he came not out again till he came to be beheaded. The rebels were put down; and then Mary, caring very little for the citizens or the people, made haste to marry the Spaniard.

But the Spaniard has gone his way; and Elizabeth's name and the name of her gallant defenders—of Grenville, Howard, Hawkins, Raleigh, Essex—and of the generals, admirals, soldiers, seamen, and navigators, have become famous, and are already denounced and hated by those who proudly pretend that to them belongs the dominion of the hitherto unknown seas, and the great golden lands beyond. Most of all is the name of one Francis Drake held in fear, for he has sailed round the world, and has struck hard at Spanish pride and cruelty in their own strongholds —performing deeds that have no parallel in history, and making the name of English adventurers words of terror in the remote garrisons of "the Indies" and the vast plains and mountain fortresses of the South.

Drake's ship, in which he circumnavigated the world, the famous *Pelican*, lies at Deptford now; and there the Queen, making a fair procession by water, and amidst the crowd of people who line the banks of the river, or lie out in barges and wherries in the stream, has accepted the invitation to a stately banquet, and Drake has been made Sir Francis. Still more years, and the *Pelican*, re-named the *Golden Hind*, has swept the coast of the Spanish main, and Drake has "singed the King of Spain's beard," and the Great Armada has borne down on England, and Elizabeth has been with the English troops at Tilbury, waiting for the foe that never came, but was swept from the sea; and so again a grand and brilliant procession comes to Ludgate. For Elizabeth comes to give thanks at St. Paul's for the great victory vouchsafed to us against our enemies. It is indeed a day of solemn thanksgiving throughout the kingdom, and one of show and state, too, and especially here on Ludgate Hill; for the Queen rides from Somerset House on a triumphal chariot or car, decked with the streamers taken from the Spaniards, and with all the great officers of her Court, lords spiritual and temporal, ladies of her household, Members of Parliament, and all the nobility and gentry. One, alas!—the great and accomplished Sir Philip Sidney —is not here, for not long ago his body was brought from Zutphen in a sad *cortége* to be buried in the church where his monument now is.

See, the Queen descends, and kneels at the great western door of the Cathedral, amidst the bishop and clergy in rich copes and vestments—while stretching away on either side to Temple Bar and the Bridge of Fleet, the City Companies, in their liveries, line the way, standing within a double railing covered with blue cloth; the Lord Mayor and sheriffs, clothed in scarlet, having received her Majesty on her entering the City. It is a splendid sight; for though the great nobility and wealthy knights have subscribed liberally to the charges of the fleet, so that the vessels that beat the Spaniards were many of them found by these private adventurers, there is great show and sumptuous apparel for the work of rejoicing. Velvet coats and doublets slashed with satin and broidered with pearls and other gems, shoes that glisten with precious stones, and hats turned up with costly jewels and rare ornaments—while the ladies in yellow ruffs and farthingales, and bodices stiff with gold and gems, attend the Queen in litters or on palfreys. All the great men here to-day have names that will be writ in the history of this land, and will live in the memories of men—in public benefactions, in the record of heroic deeds, in noble works, and in poetry, philosophy, science, and song, long after this crowd has turned to dust, and in the meaner and less heroic time to come; after Elizabeth's great heart has been gnawed by the falsehood of Essex, and she has come for the last time to Blackfriars to Lord Herbert's house to see a masque, in which she has ceased to take pleasure, but where she bears up bravely, and still dances "high and grand," though she is now old and failing. Men will speak of Spenser and Sidney, Raleigh and Cecil, Frobisher and Winter, Hawkins, Drake, Seymour, and, most of all, perhaps, of Francis Bacon, and of one other who is to stand in the forefront of the world, and yet of whom little is known at present, though we shall find him presently with Raleigh, and the wits who meet and see or hear "great things done at the 'Mermaid,'" that famous tavern of Bread Street in Chepe, where the club meets for those tournaments of fancy and of repartee which are thereafter to be associated with the name of William Shakespeare.

The Players at the Bell Savage.

among whom Shakespeare may be numbered, were probably among the privileged, for over and over again we find in the records of the earlier and middle portion of the reign of Elizabeth the City magnates denouncing and suppressing the practice of acting stage plays at inns and other public places, whereas in the older time these dramas and mysteries were only performed by the servants of the nobility at those "inns" which were private mansions, and for the amusement and moral edification of the family or of visitors, who witnessed the performance from the balconies overlooking the courtyard where the play was performed. This will perhaps explain the practice, in the earlier days of regular English dramatic art, of a company of actors or stage-players being known as "the servants" of some nobleman, who, as it were, gave them the protection of his name; and so we had the Dorset Theatre, close to Salisbury Square in Fleet Street, the Duke's, the King's, and other playhouses, while in Southwark there was the Paris Garden, the Globe, and others, some of which were devoted to bear- and bull-baiting sports, not to be suppressed while Elizabeth reigned. The great objection of the City Fathers to the players seems to have been that in many of the "inns," which were once mansions, and came to be veritable hostelries, the performance of stage plays led to much immorality, not only because of the licence of speech afforded by the drama, and its unfitness for youthful ears, or, indeed, for decent ears at all, but in consequence of the opportunities given in such places for immoral companionship. Hence we find that the players were not permitted to perform without a licence, or were only allowed on sufferance and by petition; and this appears to have been, with various vicissitudes, the condition of the drama in London—that is to say, in the City and its Liberties—until Shakespeare appears, as it were, standing in the gateway of the old Bell Savage Inn with—and we can easily fancy it—Raleigh's arm round his neck, and in his pocket a new comedy, which he is going to carry to Greenwich, Whitehall, or St. James's, to read to the Queen.

The Old Inns of London.

The transition of many old mansions into inns for public entertainment was in accordance with the changes that had taken place in other respects. The laws against vagrancy and masterless men were revived and revised, and a systematic "poor law" had been organised. Bridewell was in full swing; but so also was St. Bartholomew's, where the sick or maimed were sent for cure, and, when they had been healed, work was found for them. As to the Fleet Prison, that was full enough, and Newgate also; but, on the whole, England became under Elizabeth "a land of great and wide renown"; and there was so much show and action, earnest work and hearty play, so much intense nationality, and such a revival of letters, and also so much mirth and jollity, that it was natural even for people of consideration to meet at inns which already had a history, and there to take their ease and pleasure.

Nor was it unseemly, therefore, that those entertainments of players, morris-dancers, conjurors, and masters-of-arms, which had been held in the courtyards of private mansions should be continued in the inn yards, where the players, who had now a regular drama, could perform on a movable stage. The boys of Paul's School, too, in the age of Elizabeth act Terence and Seneca, and the choristers of Westminster and of the Queen's Chapel are called "Children of the Revels," and among them were some who had come to be fellow actors with Shakespeare, and perhaps have graced the stage of the Bell Savage. Malone, in his account of the English stage, says, "Many of our ancient dramatic pieces were performed in the yards of carriers' inns, in which, in the beginning of Queen Elizabeth's reign, the comedians who first united themselves in companies erected an occasional stage. The form of these temporary playhouses seems to be preserved in our modern theatre. The galleries in both are ranged over each other on three sides of the building. The small rooms under the lowest of these galleries answer to our present boxes; and it is observable that these, even in theatres that were built in a subsequent period expressly for dramatic exhibitions, still etained their old name, and were frequently called *rooms* by our ancient writers. The yard bears a sufficient resemblance to the pit as at present in use. We may suppose the stage to have been raised on this arena on the fourth side, with its back to the gateway of the inn, at which the money for admission was taken. Thus in fine weather a playhouse not incommodious might have been formed." So here we have Shakespeare, Burbage, Alleyn (the founder of Dulwich College) and other men famed as the representatives of English drama and poetry, come across from Southwark and the Globe and Paris Garden on Bankside to Ludgate Hill.

Shakespeare's Theatre at Blackfriars.

But they were not there only for "splitting the ears of the groundlings" at the old inn. They had purposed to have a theatre of their own close to Ludgate Hill, and there seems to have been an endeavour to avoid the persecutions which harassed the actors of that time by making it a *private* theatre, where, perhaps, the many friends and influential supporters of the "bard of Avon" maintained the drama by subscription. At all events, we find that James Burbage purchased, by deed dated February 4th, 1596, from Sir William More, of Loseley, Surrey, a large house in the Blackfriars, which he soon after converted into a theatre. In 1608 William Shakespeare had a share in the speculation, and was the proprietor of the wardrobe and properties, valued at £500. Serious complaints were made at a later date (in 1618) of the disturbance of public order and the inconvenience to the neighbourhood caused almost daily in winter time (not excepting Lent) from one or two o'clock till five at night (the usual time for christenings, burials, and afternoon service) by the playhouse being open, so that the inhabitants of Blackfriars were unable to get to the church, the ordinary passage of a great part of the precinct being close by the playhouse door. It was also represented that there was such a resort of people, and such a multitude of coaches (many of them hackney coaches, bringing people of all sorts) that they clogged up Ludgate Hill, endangered one another, broke down stalls, threw down goods, and the inhabitants were unable to get to their houses or bring in their provisions, the tradesmen to utter their wares, or passengers to get to the common water-stairs without danger of life and limb; quarrels and effusion of blood had followed, and other dangers might be occasioned by the broils, plots, and practices of such an unruly multitude. It seems to have taken about fourteen years to have vindicated the necessity for this petition, for only on November 22nd, 1633, do we find an order of the Star Chamber upon complaint of the inconvenience occasioned by the stoppage of the streets by the carriages of persons frequenting the playhouse of the Blackfriars. "Their lordships, remembering that there is an easy passage by water into that playhouse, without troubling the streets, and that it is more fit and reasonable that those which go thither should go by water or else on foot," order that all coaches shall leave as soon as they have set down, and not return till the play is over, nor return further than the west end of St. Paul's Churchyard or Fleet Conduit. Coachmen disobeying this order were to be committed to Newgate or Ludgate. Some poor pedestrians who now dread the dangers of the streets might well be excused for thinking that a week or two of the Star Chamber would do the drivers of public and even some private vehicles much good.

Land and Water.

The times were moving faster, and the conveniences of life were multiplying. One sign of change had been the introduction of coaches into England by Guilliam Boonen, a Dutchman, who became the Queen's coachman.

It is not very wonderful to find Taylor, "the water poet," denouncing this new mode of conveyance; for the Thames had been the great highway from Whitehall to the Tower, and all intermediate stations; and it was in a wherry that ladies living near the Thames went to take their airing upon the water. John Taylor, beside being a vigorous poet, author of sixty-three pieces, was a veritable waterman. He was never ashamed of his trade, though he was acquainted with Ben Jonson, and, having his boat at the

Hope Theatre, Bankside, probably did a good business, for he says—

> "But noble Thames, while I can hold a pen,
> I will divulge thy glory unto men;
> Thou, in the morning when my coin is scant,
> Before the evening doth supply my want."

But times had changed from the day when even the Lord Mayor's procession was by state barges on the noble river, where a fleet of swans sailed up and down amidst gaily-decked wherries and broad galleys, and we find Taylor saying, not without bitterness, "'Tis not fit" that

> "Fulsome madams and new scurvy squires
> Should jolt the street at pomp, at their desires;
> Like great triumphant Tamburlaines each day,
> Drawn with the pamper'd jades of Belgia;
> That almost all the streets are choked outright,
> Where men can hardly pass from morn till night,
> Whilst watermen want work."

He not unreasonably satirises the pride that led a gentlewoman to send her man to hire a coach from Ludgate Hill to carry her to see a play at the Blackfriars.

But coaches multiplied, and though the sedan chair, which was brought here by Prince Charles (afterwards Charles I.) on his return from his pretended wooing in France, superseded the *litter*, and remained a fashionable conveyance for short distances almost to within living memory—the number of public vehicles so increased that when they were limited by proclamation in 1635 there were about 1,900 in London, and in a four-miles compass of London and suburbs there were said to be 6,000, the first hackney coach *stand* having been established in 1634 by a sea captain named Baily, who set up four, with drivers in livery, to wait at the Maypole, in the Strand.

The coaches were so distasteful to the common people—partly because they made the streets dangerous, and pushed pedestrians to the wall, or constantly bespattered them with mire—that the name given them by Taylor, "hell-carts," was adopted by the populace, and they were constantly so called. The passage of Ludgate Street between the Gate and St. Paul's must have been difficult for these lumbering vehicles, except on state occasions, for there is little doubt that at one period it had what is called a middle row, or passage formed of stalls or booths erected on one side the street, with a narrow passage between them and the regular shops. But in all probability these structures were movable, and perhaps were cleared away on the occasions of processions of state or other important occasions.

Paul's Walkers—Doctors' Commons.

The narrow streets, the ill-drained houses, the want of paving, and the insufficiency of water for cleansing the city, which had expanded beyond the ancient walls, in spite of Royal proclamations against the increase of houses and the extension of the former boundaries, exposed the inhabitants to two deadly foes—fire and plague. The large quantity of timber used in building, the crowding of overhanging storeys in close thoroughfares, the inflammable materials collected in shops and warehouses, and the constant use of candles, torches, and flambeaux, made the first peril common enough, and the lack of water increased its terror. Plague was recurrent, and to this may be partly attributed the frequent acts of the City Corporation for restraining stage plays, and preventing people from assembling in large numbers for purposes of amusement within a building. The truth is that there was a great deal of legislation and much commanding and proclaiming; but that did not prevent a vast amount of disorder. St. Paul's Cathedral was in a disgraceful condition, for it had become a promenade and general resort for loungers, idlers, and persons whose characters were by no means unquestionable. It had always had this disgraceful reputation in former times, and even as early as the reign of Edward III. there were complaints of the kind, while in the reign of Richard III. the scandal continued, even though excommunication had been pronounced against the offenders. Indeed, the marketing, gossiping, lounging and making of assignations in St. Paul's came to be defended as ancient usages, and in the reign of Philip and Mary the church was a common passage-way for conveying all kinds of merchandise, including beer, bread, fish, and meat, and mules, horses, and cattle were actually led through the building. After the Reformation many of these indecencies continued, and the condition of the grand old Cathedral is frequently suggested by the dramatists and poets of that age. Before, and even after, the building of the Royal Exchange by Sir Thomas Gresham, and its inauguration by the Queen herself, who dined with the eminent merchant on the occasion at his house in Bishopsgate, the church was used as a commercial mart, and bills or advertisements were fastened to the columns in the aisles.

Among the curious notices relating to the irreverent practices pursued in this church in the time of Elizabeth, collected by Mr. Malcolm from the manuscript presentments or visitations preserved at St. Paul's, are found that, "in the upper quier, wher the common [communion] table dothe stande, there is much unreverente people *walking* with their *hatts on their heddes* commonly all the service time, no man reproving them for yt." And also, "Yt is greate disorder in the church, that porters, butchers, and water-bearers, and who not, be suffered (in special time of service) to carrye and recarrye whatsoever, no man withstandinge them or gainsaying them."

The middle of St. Paul's was, in fact, the Bond Street of the period—if, indeed, we can now realise what Bond Street was when it was regarded as a daily resort in the time of George IV. Up to the time of the Commonwealth the young gallants from the Inns of Court, and others who desired to make a show of spirit and fashion, used to meet at the central point of St. Paul's, and were known as "Paul's Walkers"; just as in the last generation some men were known as "Bond Street Loungers." However strange it may seem, tradition says that the great Lord Bacon in his youth was one of them. Many of them were poor enough, and they, along with other impecunious frequenters of the place, were said to go there at mid-day "to diné with Duke Humphrey"—a proverb which originated in the fact that one of the chief meeting-places was at the only conspicuous monument near the screen of the altar, really the monument of Sir John Beauchamp, one of the House of Warwick already mentioned, but erroneously supposed to be that of

Humphrey, the good Duke of Gloucester—before which the poor visitors used to strew herbs and sprinkle water. The high altar no longer shone resplendent as in the days before the Reformation, nor were there throngs of priests and choristers mingling with the visitors, or making processions in the aisles. Several other tombs were added, however, the most prominent being that of Sir Christopher Hatton, whose high and stately dancing * was said to have won the admiration of Elizabeth, who subsequently made him her Chancellor; or, as Gray says of him,—

> "His bushy beard, and shoe-strings green,
> His high crown'd hat and satin doublet,
> Mov'd the stout heart of England's Queen,
> Though Pope and Spaniard could not trouble it."

Another of Elizabeth's great statesmen lay there also—Walsingham, who died so deeply in debt that his body was secretly buried, lest it should be seized by his creditors. Sir Christopher Hatton, too, is said to have died broken-hearted because his royal mistress exacted from him a debt which he found it difficult to pay; and we may, therefore, understand that all the great show and state was not maintained without cost, and that the extravagant dress, and jewelled shoes and hats, were, after all, paid for—if not in coin, in anxiety and care. The tomb of Chancellor Hatton so eclipsed those of Sir Philip Sidney and Walsingham by its size and pretentiousness, and its long, pompous, and rather absurd epitaph, that old Stow made an epigram on it, which has been often quoted as a legend of St. Paul's,—

> " Philip and Francis have no tomb,
> For great Christopher takes all the room."

Many changes were made in Ludgate Hill and its neighbourhood. The old gate was not only repaired, but rebuilt; the statues of King Lud and his sons placed in a niche on the east side; and on the west front the statue of the Queen herself was placed in 1586.

Doctors' Commons, on the Hill of St. Bennet, just behind Great Knightrider Street, may be said to have been begun

* The dancing of that period consisted in high steps, leaps, and posing of the figure.

in the reign of Elizabeth, for though, as people found to their cost, the ecclesiastical lawyers who held courts within the jurisdiction of the Church were numerous and powerful enough in the time of Henry VII., and had grown so overbearing in the next reign that Cranmer set himself to reduce the number of proctors (or attorneys), and to bring the Courts into something like order, there were still a large number of civil cases which were brought under ecclesiastical law. Doctors' Commons was, in fact, a college or common-house for doctors of law, and for the study and practice of the law. Cardinal Wolsey had intended to build a college of stone, for the purpose of receiving the community; but his fortunes waned, and it was not till the early part of the reign of Elizabeth that Master Henry Harvey, Doctor of the Civil and Canon Laws, Master of Trinity Hall, Cambridge, Prebendary of Ely, and Dean of the Arches, succeeded in taking the lawyers and Canonists from their rather mean lodgings in Paternoster Row, in a house which afterwards became the Queen's Head Tavern, and procuring for them a lease of a large building, formerly the house of Lord Mountjoy.

After the Fire of London, which swept away the old College, the doctors, proctors, and advocates met at Essex House till the new building was finished—a brick-fronted structure, of the kind that prevailed immediately after the Fire, with an interior consisting of two quadrangles, chiefly occupied by the doctors, a hall for the hearing of causes, a spacious library, a refectory, and other apartments. The Admiralty Court was of great importance in later times, and the judge was distinguished by being preceded as he went into Court by an usher carrying a silver oar.

In our own day, however, Doctors' Commons has been most famous for the Matrimonial and Wills Courts. The Bank of England acknowledged no wills that had not been proved there, and the enormous number of wills searched in the Prerogative Will Office, and the wills there deposited have been of the greatest importance, not only for determining the succession of various families, but in order to verify the personal history of famous individuals. Shakespeare's will, in three folio sheets, each signed in proper legal form, the will of Vandyck (the Court painter to Charles I., who lived and died in the precinct), of Inigo Jones, Sir Isaac Newton, of John Milton, Edmund Burke, and formerly (for it was sent to Paris at the request of the late Emperor), the will of Napoleon I. were all deposited here. Each folio of Shakespeare's will is on a polished oak frame, and kept in an air-tight space between two sheets of plate glass. The original wills begin with the year 1483, and the copies from 1383, and the more ancient, mostly on strong parchment bound in clasped volumes, are, or were, allowed to be inspected on permission obtained from the Judge of the Court of Probate, who will also allow extracts to be copied for historical purposes.

The marriage licences, however, have been less carefully preserved, or at all events they have none earlier than 1632, and until 1695 they are not complete. But the very name of Doctors' Commons will soon be either lost or perverted. There is virtually an end to all that made either the place or its practice truly distinctive. The Probate, Divorce, and Admiralty Division of the High Court of Justice has absorbed its functions, and perhaps by the time the building of the new Law Courts is finished, only the memory of the *habitué* will be able to discover the once well-known places where the advocates from Oxford sat in scarlet and taffety, and those from Cambridge in minever and round black velvet caps.

Yet it is worth while to plunge into the nest of steep lanes that lie on the "bow" side of the yard. We are sure to come upon some quaint remnant of former state, some building only half demolished which tells a scrap of history, some antique nook or corner that may remind us how clumsy are the innovators who think they are improvers, and who begin by destroying the truly old and venerable, instead of the commonplace and sordid adjuncts of an historic neighbourhood, till the chandler's shop blots out the heraldic blazonry of some palace gateway, and the solemn vestibule of a forgotten court or a prelate's hall of judgment crumbles in ruin behind the stall of a greengrocer or the dimly-lighted shed of a retail coal merchant.

There is a glamour about heraldry which gives it an

appearance of antiquity; but, as matter of fact, the devices borne by the early warriors were but the badges, the distinctive signs, afterwards associated with the motto or war-cries assumed by leaders or great families who took the field with their followers, and had a crest or design by which they and their retainers might be known—just as the Plantagenets bore a branch of broom, or the Houses of York and Lancaster took the white and red roses for their caps. The heralds, who were, in fact, only messengers on the field or at the tournaments, were acquainted with these distinctive emblems, but it was at a late date that they had any authority to pronounce on the right of the wearers to assume them. There was, in fact, no heraldic science till the reign of Edward III., and the Heralds' College, or College of Arms, was founded by Richard II. at Cold Harbour House, Poultney Lane, whence it was removed by Henry VII., that Bishop Tunstal might have the place for a mansion after he had been turned out of Durham House. It was not till Mary, in 1555, gave Gilbert Dethick, Garter King-at-Arms, and his heralds and pursuivants the building on the east side of Bennet's Hill, that the College may be said to have been established, and by that time the adoption of coats-of-arms by the leaders who had originated them had led to a formal record of shields, crests, and quarterings.

After the Great Fire, from which the books and records of the College of Arms were saved, it seemed as though the officials would find no home, for the City's cash had to be spent for more immediately practical purposes, and only about £700 was raised by subscription; but the amount required to rebuild was taken from the office fees, and Sir William Dugdale, Garter King-at-Arms, most learned and enthusiastic of antiquaries, author of the great *Monasticon Anglicanum*, built the north-west portion at his own charge. The present quaint but spacious and handsome building, brought into the main thoroughfare by the extensive changes that have been made by opening up Queen Victoria Street to Blackfriars, is one of the most complete relics now remaining of London immediately after the Great Fire. It is so peculiarly fresh and sharp in all its architectural details that we are almost surprised to find so much that is really ancient in its repositories; far more ancient are the monuments and curiosities to be found there than the escutcheons bearing the arms—or rather legs—of the Isle of Man, and the eagle claw of the house of Stanley, which denotes that it is on the site of old Derby House. There are, for instance, a pedigree of the Saxon kings from Adam, illustrated with many fine pen-and-ink drawings, executed in the time of Henry VIII.; the "Warwick Roll," with a series of the figures of all the Earls of Warwick from the Conquest to the reign of Richard III.; the roll of the Tournament at Westminster held in honour of Queen Katherine after the birth of Prince Henry; the sword, dagger, and turquoise ring of the gallant James IV. of Scotland, who was slain on Flodden Field, and a great collection of papers, certificates, and historical MSS. If for no other reason, the College of Arms commands the respect even of the most obstinate objector to the heraldic science because of the number of eminent men who held high office there. The principal staff consists of three Kings-at-Arms —Garter, Clarencieux, and Norroy; six heralds—Somerset, Richmond, Lancaster, Windsor, Chester, and York; and four pursuivants—Rouge Dragon, Blue Mantle, Portcullis, and Rouge Croix. All these offices are in the gift of the Duke of Norfolk, Hereditary Grand Marshal, and among the famous Kings-at-Arms have been William Camden, author of the learned and interesting *Britannica* and *Annals of Elizabeth;* Sir William Le Neve; Elias Ashmole, the founder of the Ashmolean Museum; Dugdale, the great antiquary already mentioned; Sir John Vanbrugh, wit and dramatist; Francis Grose, author of Grose's *Antiquities;* and William Oldys, the queer little fellow who spent most of his evenings at the Bell Tavern in the Old Bailey, was rather too fond of porter, and is now chiefly known for the Anacreontic verse on a fly drinking from his cup of ale,—

> "Busy, curious, thirsty fly,
> Drink with me, and drink as I;
> Freely welcome to my cup,
> Couldst thou sip, and sip it up.
> Make the most of life you may;
> Life is short, and wears away.

> "Both alike are mine and thine
> Hastening quick to their decline;
> Thine's a summer, mine no more,
> Though repeated to threescore;
> Threescore summers, when they're gone,
> Will appear as short as one."

We cannot, however, omit one more name, well known to the past generation, that of James Robinson Planché, Somerset Herald, whose delightful extravaganzas, as charming for their versification and their wit as for the superb manner in which they were placed upon the stage, made the great attraction of the Lyceum Theatre under the management of Madame Vestris. It is but a few years ago that Mr. Planché passed away, at a ripe old age, still distinguished for his ready humour, his facile pen, and for the charm of his social qualities.

There were great transitions during the time of Elizabeth, and many changes came over Ludgate Hill and its neighbourhood. Among other imposing landmarks, the high campanile, or bell-tower, by St. Paul's School, disappeared when Sir Miles Partridge won it from Henry VIII. at a throw of dice, and promptly took it down and sold the materials—perhaps lest his imperious debtor should revoke the stakes.

But the age of Bacon and of Raleigh, of Spenser and of Shakespeare, was one of progress.

In a very definite sense the people, and especially the citizens of London and the "men of light and leading," were brought nearer together, and to this the conversion of many old buildings into public inns and hostelries doubtless contributed, for it was here that many of the amusements in which all classes participated were carried on. The old Bell Savage held a prominent position in this respect, and Ludgate Hill and its immediate neighbourhood was a centre both of the intellectual and the social life of that period. It is true that some of the amusements were not very refined, but they will mostly bear comparison with many that are familiar to ourselves. We might not tolerate such an exhibition as that of the ascent of a horse to the top of St. Paul's Cathedral, a feat performed by the famous nag Marocco, whose fame, with that of Bankes, his master, has lived in every history of the time, and was even alluded to by Shakespeare himself in *Love's Labour's Lost*, where Moth, to prove the simplicity of a certain problem in arithmetic, says, "The dancing horse will tell you." It was in 1595 that all London was crowding to Ludgate Hill to see this famous animal, who was a young chestnut or bay nag, trained to perform such tricks as to walk on its hind legs and gravely to dance "The Canaries," to carry a glove to any person indicated by its master, such as the gentleman in the large ruff, or the lady with the green hood. It would count coins by raps of its feet, tell the number of a cast of dice, and occasionally assist in such jocularities as singling out the gentleman who was in love, or the lady who was waiting for a lover. Along with Bankes and his horse, the Bell Savage was often visited by the famous clown or jester Tarleton, who was landlord of Dolly's Tavern, in Paternoster Row. Tarleton was the prototype of the circus clowns and most of the other jesters of our day, and his witticisms were the constant talk of the town, for which he provided quips and popular sayings. A book of his jests ("Tarleton's Jest Booke") was published, and the order of his wit was about equal to that of the "bones" of the negro troupes, or the best of the circus clowns of to-day, but, in the manner of the earlier jesters, sometimes contained grave and suggestive allusions to state affairs, or the doings of great persons. During the period of Elizabeth, and to the time of the Commonwealth, when theatres, stage plays, and public shows were put down by the sterner Puritans, and public amusements would have been suppressed altogether but for the interposition of Cromwell, Ludgate Hill and Fleet Street as far as Temple Bar was the great show-place of London, for it was the centre, the highway from Whitehall and the Strand, where the Maypole stood by St. Mary's Church, to the Tower and the great trading neighbourhoods of Chepe, Grass Church, Leadenhall, and Mart Lane. But it was, as we have seen, the centre of ecclesiastical rule and of learning also, and this was made more obvious by the establishment of

STATIONERS' HALL.

We have already noted that Paternoster Row and the neighbourhood of Ludgate had become the quarter whence learning was disseminated by means of books, and it is well to remember that the title of Stationers was at that time applied almost exclusively to booksellers, and that this meaning continued to be attached to it until the beginning of the last century. It signified a person who had a station, or stall, in some public place for the sale of books, and in the middle ages was applied to the official who sold at a stall the books written for the particular university with which he was connected.

The Stationers' Company, which, though it is distinguished by being the only London company restricted to members of the craft implied by its name, now consists of dealers in the *material* for making books, as well as of *booksellers*, was incorporated in the reign of Philip and Mary, and for nearly two centuries had, so to speak, a monopoly of the means of learning. Printers were obliged to serve an apprenticeship to a member of the company, and every book or printed matter published—"from a bible to a ballad," as Peter Cunningham says—was required to be entered at Stationers' Hall. Now, the company publishes nothing but almanacks, of which, till the last few years, they had a monopoly; and Old Moore's Almanack, which is the imitation of a farrago by Lilly, the pretended astrologer, who lived near, in Shoe Lane, in the time of Charles II., was one of their great sources of income. It is not now necessary to enter publications at Stationers' Hall; but, by the Copyright Act, the proprietor of every published work must register his claim to it in the books of the company if he wishes to protect himself before taking legal proceedings for piracy or imitation. The company soon had a local habitation, as well as a name. Their first hall appears to have been in Milk Street, Cheapside, and in 1553 they removed to St. Peter's College, near St. Paul's Deanery, where the chantry priests of the Cathedral had formerly lived. Between Amen Corner and Ludgate Street, at the end of a passage from Ave Maria Lane, in the same spot now occupied by Stationers' Hall, stood a great house of stone and wood which, in the days of Edward III., belonged to John, Duke of Bretagne and Earl of Richmond. From him it went to the Earl of Pembroke, and was called

Pembroke's Inn, and then came into possession of the family of Henry Nevill, Lord of Abergavenny, and was known as Burgavenny House. This was the place where the Stationers' Company was located in 1611 (James I.), and here, in another building erected on the same place, after the old Inn was burnt in the Fire of London, the honourable guild holds state to-day. Property to the value of £200,000 was lost by the Stationers' Company in the Great Fire, but their priceless records are still most interesting, consisting chiefly of the enormously extensive register of works for publication, which may be said to be an index to English literature from 1557, the date at which it commences.

The Stationers' Company has been famous, like some other guilds, for its festivals, and particularly for its venison feast, founded in 1659, and held in the large and handsome hall, with its raised daïs, its fine window, and its buffets or cupboards full of numerous articles of quaint and valuable plate, collected since the Great Fire, in which all their former possessions of this kind were destroyed. That which now remains is chiefly of the time of Charles II. In the Hall have been seen some remarkable meetings, and many of them are historical, such as the St. Cecilian Feast, in 1697, for which Dryden wrote "Alexander's Feast," afterwards set to music by Handel, in 1736; the Reform Banquet to Lord Althorp and Lord John Russell, in 1831; and others, among which have been some funeral celebrations of great state and magnificence. The chief attraction of the Hall to visitors is the interesting and admirable collection of portraits that adorn the walls; including those of Steele, Richardson, Prior, Pope, and Dr. Hoadley, Bishop of Bangor, Steele's friend and decorously festive companion. It was at an anniversary banquet at the Hall one day that one of the inferior officers of the company, who was know as a humourist, but who on that occasion was "half seas over," came in on his knees to drink to the "glorious memory." Everybody present was pretty far gone, Steele included, and Hoadley was rather disconcerted when the genial writer and wit whispered to him, "Do laugh, my lord; pray laugh; 'tis *humanity* to laugh," and the good-humoured prelate broke into a chuckle. Steele sent him an apology next day, in which the following couplet must have been sufficient acknowledgment of the grace of the reverend bishop,—

"Virtue with so much ease on Bangor sits,
All faults he pardons, though he none commits."

We can scarcely dismiss our recollections of the educational agencies about Ludgate Hill without thinking for a moment of the College of Physicians; not the present fine building in Pall Mall East, but the old one in Warwick Lane, and the still older one in Knightrider Street, in the house of Linacre, the founder of the college, and physician to Henry VIII. It was on the site of No. 5, Knightrider Street, that Linacre lived, and that spot is worthily distinguished by the house being still the property of the College. It was not till (1564) after the accession of Elizabeth that dissections were permitted; and when the first lectures were commenced in 1583, a large anatomical theatre was built adjoining the house. Here it was that the great Harvey first lectured; but the College, at about the time Charles I. succeeded to the throne, moved to a house belonging to the Dean and Chapter of St. Paul's, at the farther end of Amen Corner, where they built another theatre, and planted a botanical garden, which occupied ground going as far west as the Old Bailey, and skirting behind the houses of Ludgate Street, as far as St. Martin's Church. Here was the fine library to which Selden, Ashmole, Sir Theodore Mayerne, and others contributed such a valuable collection of books. But the building was swept away in the conflagration of the following year, and only 112 folio volumes of all the library were saved. Then the College left the site of building and garden for the erection of houses for the clergy of St. Paul's, and bought a plot of ground in Warwick Lane, where a new building was erected, and opened in 1674—a quaint old brick and stone structure with which, as the College of Physicians, many of us were once familiar, though it had long since ceased to have any connection with its original design, and was hustled and profaned by the greasy sheds and shambles of Newgate Market.

SWORD, PLAGUE, FIRE, AND REVOLUTION.

There is no need to follow all the subsequent legends of Ludgate Hill during the reign of the Stuarts. When James I. was ready to be crowned, the plague had been rife in London, and there was no great procession; but the King began by knighting everybody all round, and the Lord Mayor and Aldermen had a good time of it at the Coronation Banquet, a circumstance which was probably remembered when the King went a-borrowing in the City. It was a sad time, and Bartholomew Fair was closed, the theatres were forbidden, and the yard of the Old Bell Savage was unusually silent; but the distemper having ceased, the pageants and feasting and brave shows began, and Ludgate was alive again with a magnificent procession, wherein the King "rode a white gennet under a rich canopy upheld by six gentlemen of the Privy Council." But there was another kind of procession not long after—a dark and wretched train, moving slowly under the shadow of the scaffold erected at the west front of St. Paul's, for Sir Everard Digby, Robert Winter, John Grant, and Thomas Bates, for their share in the Gunpowder Plot. Next day, Guy Fawkes, Thomas Winter, Ambrose Rockwood, and Robert Key met a similar fate at Old Palace Yard, and the quartered bodies and severed heads of these unhappy wretches were seen upon the City gates, or on poles on London Bridge, a gruesome spectacle. The great festivals, processions, and splendid pageants prepared for the visit of Christian IV. of Denmark took away the scent of the blood, for the conduits ran wine, and were adorned with pretty pastoral devices and bowers, where songs were sung and orations were made, and down the hill through Ludgate passed a splendid train of Danish and English nobles.

The reign of the first James was a lively time for Ludgate. The Inns were in full swing. Ben Jonson had his Apollo Club at the Devil Tavern, by Temple Bar, and there was goodly company all round. Burbage and Shakespeare had obtained their theatre at Blackfriars in spite of the opposition of the Civic Council, and Fleet Street was full of shows, some burlesque indication of which may be found in Jonson's *Every Man in His Humour*, where it speaks of "a new motion of the City of Nineveh, with Jonah and the Whale at Fleet Bridge." Down to a comparatively modern date these shows continued, and were at their height in the reign of Queen Anne. The last of them may still be remembered by some of our older readers—by name, at all events—as Mrs. Salmon's collection of waxwork, at the "former palace of Henry VIII. and Cardinal Wolsey," opposite Chancery Lane, which, by-the-bye, was neither a palace nor a residence of either the King or his Minister, but the office of the Duchy of Cornwall in the reign of James I., and perhaps the house built by Sir Amyas Paulet. Before Mrs. Salmon took it, it was "Nando's," a famous coffee-house frequented by the barristers of the Temple.

Our gossip has already carried us from the days of doublet and trunk hose, of ruff and farthingale, and indeed we need not dwell upon the times that followed the reign of the Royal pedant. Nor is there occasion to do more than refer the reader to Sir Walter Scott's "Fortunes of Nigel" to discover how lawless the neighbourhood of the Fleet Ditch had by that time become, and how between the Temple and Bridewell lay the Alsatia of London, occupying the steep and crooked lanes and sinks that then made the foul district of Whitefriars. We come now to royal domination, popular resistance, plague, the stocks, the pillory, and the whipping-post, courtly magnificence, a decorous royal family, licentious and unscrupulous favourites, a Church exceedingly militant, and everywhere the element of organised revolt on the one hand, and of hot resistance to the demand for Constitutional government on the other.

St. Paul's Church had taken a new aspect, for the restorations begun by James I. were finished, and Inigo Jones had added to the great rugged structure a splendid but absurdly incongruous portico at the Western front. It consisted of fourteen Corinthian columns, rising to the height of forty-six feet, and so disposed that eight with two pilasters placed in front and three on each side formed an oblong square peristyle, and supported an entablature and balustrade in which were the statues of the royal predecessors of Charles I. The whole of the body of the Church had been cased with rustic work, so that the ancient details were obliterated, and only the general forms and proportions left; and some of the windows were fitted with Italian decorations, so that the "restoration" was a confusing and anomalous performance. But the march and tramp of armed men again sounds on Ludgate Hill. The grim, ungracious warriors of the Commonwealth are clanking in the streets, and the reign of the sectaries has begun by sweeping away show and pageant and stage play. Laughter and jest are hushed for the moment at the old inns and at the City feasts. Men look grave, and begin to count the number of courses, and to wonder whether there shall be no more cakes and ale. Yet there must be amusements, and the shops and stalls about Ludgate find customers even among the Parliamentary soldiers, who take up their quarters, not only in the inns and taverns, but elsewhere. St. Paul's Churchyard echoes with the noise of these troopers playing at ninepins, and at unseasonable hours, too; and they and their comrades show so little respect for the grand old cathedral that its destruction seems almost imminent. Some scaffolding set up for repairing the building has been made over to them for arrears of pay, and they take it down so hurriedly that part of the vaulting falls in and lies in a heap. They dig pits in the body of the church to use as saw-pits for converting this timber into saleable lengths, and their barracks and stables occupy another portion of the cathedral, so that only the east end and a part of the choir are used for public worship, a brick wall having been raised to separate them from the rest of the building, the congregation entering and departing by one of the northern windows. Inigo Jones's magnificent portico is occupied with milliners' and other shops, to construct which and to make lodgings above them the ends of beams are let into the superb Corinthian columns. Of course, the statues of the kings are tumbled down and broken, and unless some change should occur the whole edifice will be a heap of ruins.

A change comes with the Restoration, when all the bells in London are ringing, and the streets are gay again with tapestries and rich mats and carpets hung from balconies and windows. The conduits flow with wine, and through

Lud Gate (which was somewhat defaced when other gates and portcullises were destroyed by order of the Rump Parliament, before General Monk found out that he must conciliate the City), rides Charles II. between his two brothers, the Dukes of York and Gloucester, and attended by a gorgeous cavalcade. There are amusements enough now; and though Shakespeare and Ben Jonson are no longer in Blackfriars, the yard of the Bell Savage is open to the merry-andrews, jack-puddings, and rope-dancers, while new playhouses are opened in Dorset Gardens, in Lincoln's Inn, Salisbury Court, Holborn, and other places; but the plays are full of immoral allusions, and the audience has already caught the licence and the immodesty of the Court.

But again these houses are closed; public assemblies are forbidden, and the whole City is wrapped in gloom, for once more the plague has begun its ravages, and the dismal cry of "Bring out your dead!" and the rumble of the cart that comes to convey corpses to the dreadful pits that have been dug around the confines of the populous neighbourhoods sounds like a nightly dirge in the dark and nearly-deserted streets, where fires of coal and bitumen flare in braziers, and cast a lurid glare upon the dreadful scene. Defoe tells us that 100,000 people died of the plague only in that one year 1665, and it was believed that 10,000 were saved by going to live in boats and barges on the river. The King and Court went to Oxford, and there was much hurrying from the City; but amidst it all old gossiping Pepys seems to have kept his head, and to have gone about his business steadily, after sending his wife to Woolwich, which was, so to speak, in his official beat as he had so often to go to Deptford about the business of the Fleet. There was little known of the disease from which the people were suffering, and the deaths went on increasing until some atmospheric change seems to have occurred. The plague was no new thing. It had been recurrent in London for ages, though some improvements had taken place, and a better water supply had been obtained since 1580, when Peter Morris, the Dutchman, had set up huge water-wheels at London Bridge, which, moved by the rapid tide, became a motive power to force the water through wooden tubes to the conduits; a method which lasted till nearly the end of the last century, and did not, even in conjunction with Sir Hugh Myddelton's scheme, supersede the water-carriers, who plied their trade from the conduits even in the time of William III.

There was only one remedy for the plague, as it seemed, and that was the destruction of the nests of infection which propagated, if they did not originate, it. The plague was stayed by fire, and with the Great Fire of 1666 the Legends of Ludgate Hill take a new phase. The old buildings of which we have recounted the story disappeared, and where once was a great, ancient, and wealthy city stood a vast smouldering plain, dotted in complex lines and confusing ranks with heaps of ruins. The people bore it bravely, living in huts in the fields outside the large space where once arose churches, mansions, towers, warehouses, palaces, and marts. Merchants kept to their engagements, and carried on their business with dogged, painstaking patience. Never was English endurance and English courage more strikingly manifested than in the manner in which this vast calamity was borne; never was English energy and determination more signally exemplified than in the fact that in little more than four years another London had arisen from the ashes of the former one—and perhaps too closely on the foundations of that which had perished—for in spite of the advice and the desire of the great architect, who seemed himself to be an embodiment of the energy and pluck of the nation, the new London, instead of opening out with broad thoroughfares and a great river enbankment and fine streets, with the Cathedral as a centre, was built much on the old lines. It was a restoration; and so, where church and hall and college and mansion had fallen, new buildings rose with the same names and purposes, and Ludgate and the Hill, Newgate and the Fleet, and Bridewell and the old Bell Savage stood there yet, what had been left of the latter to be restored into a venerable inn, soon to receive into its capacious yard the coaches which were to open up the country to Londoners, and to awaken the echoes of the streets with the lumbering clatter of their wheels. But only the nucleus of the present capital then existed. There were no lines of warehouses and immense

LUDGATE DURING THE GREAT FIRE.

docks for shipping between the Tower and Blackwall. Chelsea was a country village. There were no stately mansions extending far beyond Whitehall and Westminster. Over the site of the borough of Marylebone, and over the greater part of the space now covered by the boroughs of Finsbury and the Tower Hamlets, sportsmen wandered with dog and gun, and cattle roamed and fed.

Sir Christopher Wren had been appointed surveyor-general and principal architect, and he had planned out a new City, with enlarged streets and lanes, carrying them as nearly parallel as might be; avoiding, if compatible with greater convenience, all acute angles. All the parochial churches were to be conspicuous and insular; the most public places were to be large piazzas, the centre of six or eight ways; the halls of the twelve chief City companies were to be united in one regular square annexed to Guildhall, and a quay or esplanade was to be made on the whole river bank from Blackfriars to the Tower. The streets were to be of three magnitudes, the three principal leading straight through the City, and one or two cross streets to be at least ninety feet wide, others sixty feet, and lanes about thirty feet, excluding all narrow, dark alleys without thoroughfares, and all courts. But the enormous increasing value of land in the City, the rigid conservatism of the owners of property, and the cry of "vested interests" prevented the scheme from being executed, and—here we are—slowly and at enormous cost gradually assimilating the City to something like the plan advised above two centuries ago. But if the plan was rejected, the style of building was vastly improved, so far as ordinary houses and dwellings were concerned. The ordinary material was brick of a good quality. On the sites of the ancient parish churches had arisen a multitude of new domes, towers, and spires, which bore the marks of the fertile genius of Wren. In every place save one the traces of the great devastation had been completely effaced. But the crowds of workmen, the scaffolds, and the masses of hewn stone were still to be seen when the noblest of Protestant temples was slowly rising on the ruins of the old Cathedral of St. Paul.*

* Macaulay.

To give an account of the Great Fire it would be only necessary to make copious extracts from Evelyn and dear old amusing Pepys; but their books are now within the reach of every reader of cheap editions. It is to be noted that while all Ludgate and the Hill and the surrounding thoroughfares were in cinders, the gate of Lud was little injured—even the statue of Elizabeth, the figures of Lud and his sons, and the coat-of-arms being but slightly damaged.

The Church of St. Martin, Ludgate, of course, was burnt. It was one of the most ancient (some said *the* most ancient) in London, for it was declared that Cadwallo, the ancient British king, was buried here in a former church. The one destroyed by the Fire was dated 1437, and was a fine building, with two projecting porches in Ludgate Hill, and a curious spire. The new church stands farther back than the old. The little black spire that adorns the tower rises from a small bulb of a cupola, round which runs a light gallery. Between the street and the body of the church Wren, always ingenious, contrived an ambulatory the whole depth of the tower, to deaden the sound of passing traffic. The church is a cube, the length 57 feet, the breadth 66 feet; the spire, 168 feet high, is dwarfed by St. Paul's. The building cost in erection £5,378 18s. 8d.

The font, the gift of Thomas Morley, in 1673, is encircled with an old Greek palindrome, or line which reads the same both ways, and means

"Cleanse thy sins, not merely thy outward self."

An old carved seat and some ornamented chests in the vestry room are of the date 1690. Perhaps the Church of St. Martin Ludgate is most famous for the fact that, in 1613, the famous Samuel Purchas was rector there. He was the editor of "Hakluyt's Voyages," and brought them into his "Pilgrims," a work of five folio volumes, full of accounts of travels and adventures.

It is said that Wren designed the present slender spire of St. Martin's to give a greater importance to the dome of St. Paul's, before which it stands as we look up Ludgate Hill from one point of view. Coleridge used to compare a certain gentleman, who was always putting himself forward to explain Mr. Fox's sentiments, to the steeple of St. Martin, which is always getting in the way when you want to look at St. Paul's.

There is one familiar building which has had an association with Ludgate Hill ever since the reconstruction of London, but it is not a restoration. It is original, and was erected in 1670, marking "a new departure" in the practice of physic. Apothecaries' Hall, in Water Lane, Blackfriars, at once elevated the druggists' business to a professional status by providing the Apothecaries' Company (incorporated by charter in the reign of James I.) with a hall and a dispensary. Originally the physicians formed a part of the Apothecaries' Company, but professional jealousies and the demand of the apothecaries not only to dispense, but to prescribe, brought them into conflict. It may be mentioned that students at the hospitals still go up to pass an examination at Apothecaries' Hall, where they are often asked questions on surgery, or rather on what surgery was a generation ago, so that some of the queries are out of the line of modern practice; and that they are expected to be able to read and explain some of the prescriptions, yellow with age, which may have been almost identical with those of Radcliffe, Lettsom, or Garth. The quarrel between the physicians and the apothecaries began by the latter gradually superseding the "regular practitioners," who retaliated by commencing to see "gratis patients," who took the prescriptions to the apothecaries to be "made up." Then the physicians accused their opponents of making extortionate charges, and though the apothecaries indignantly denied it, and offered to adopt a scale settled by a committee of physicians, it was decided to sell drugs and to dispense medicines at the College of Physicians at cost price; an unjust proceeding which ended in long litigation, and, before the claim of the apothecaries was settled by law, to a bitter quarrel, not only between apothecaries and physicians, but between physicians themselves, who were divided into dispensarians and anti-dispensarians. The famous Sir Samuel Garth was one of the former, and his famous satire, "'The Dispensary," shows us a great deal of the pretty quarrel with the apothecaries, of whose Hall he says:—

> " Nigh where Fleet Ditch descends in sable streams,
> To wash the sooty naiads of the Thames,
> There stands a structure on a rising hill,
> Where tyros take their freedom out to kill."

The poem is graphic enough, and abounds with bitter and unsparing satire, which must have told heavily at the time, but it is now almost forgotten, and there are few "apothecaries" practising as such, though the modern "chemist" is often accused of illegally assuming the prerogative of the physician, instead of merely discharging the duty of the dispenser, and "practitioners" in poor neighbourhoods are opening shops for giving "medical advice" and selling medicines under the name of "dispensaries." Thus "history repeats itself," even in its less prominent and striking features.

The old "Surgeons' Hall," or College of Surgeons, which every reader of Smollett will remember, was in the Old Bailey, and it was here that Oliver Goldsmith, who was then living in a court close by, was rejected in his examination for a surgeon's mate. Had he passed we should probably never have had the "Vicar of Wakefield," or the "Deserted Village."

The improvement in the public health by the rebuilding of London can scarcely be over-estimated, but we find it difficult to realise the condition of the streets and the means of locomotion at that time, and even to a much later date. The pavement was detestable, and at night many of the footways were dangerous, and the drainage was so imperfect that in rainy weather the gutters, especially those which roared and gurgled their "disemboguing streams" into Fleet Ditch, were torrents, and foot passengers were bespattered with the evil-smelling mud by the broad wheels of carts and coaches lumbering past. Ben Jonson, Dryden, Pope, Swift, and nearly all the satirists have launched their denunciations against Fleet Ditch, as the river came to be called, and not a few of them have told us in striking language what was the condition of the thoroughfares near at hand. In the narrow streets the sedan chair was the favourite conveyance; and no wonder. Only people robustly shod could walk except in very fine weather, and though after the rebuilding the thoroughfares were wider and the coaches became wider also, while the driver could sit on a box, instead of on a low bar or astride his horse, the dangers of the streets were very considerable. It must be remembered, too, that public games were still played in the open spaces, and that it was no uncommon event for a football party to come rushing down from the Strand. It was necessary for safety to " take the wall " side of the pavement, and keep as far from the road as possible ; but the wall was mostly taken by the bully, by the butcher, greasy from Newgate Market, or the sweep, sooty from a court in the Old Bailey. If two bullies or roysterers met they cocked their hats in each other's faces, and had a tussle till one of them was shoved into the kennel. The rule of the pavement—keeping to the right—as it is practised, or should be practised, in our time, was unobserved, and indeed the dangers of the edge of the pathway were imminent. Strong posts to protect the pedestrian from cart and coach wheels, or to form landmarks to prevent him from sousing into the gutter on dark nights, were absolutely necessary. From the roofs and gutters a flood often descended, and close overhead creaked innumerable signs, which added to the picturesque appearance of the City more than to its safety or convenience. The houses were not numbered, and the signs were necessary where porters, coachmen, errand boys, and chairmen had never learnt to read. The painted boards, therefore, projected from shopfronts, not from taverns or inns merely, but even from the booksellers' in St. Paul's Churchyard and Paternoster Row. At night the danger and difficulty of walking in the streets was increased. Not only were thieves and bullies lying in wait at dark corners, but more unscrupulous and more terrifying ruffians, who called themselves " men of spirit " and gentlemen, played their pranks by night—upset coaches, prodded quiet and feeble men with their swords, assaulted women, and even invented tortures and ill-usage for the weak and the defenceless who came in their way. They had various names, and there was a regular succession of high-life scoundrelism, from the Muns and Tityre Tus to the Hectors, and in later times the Scourers, the Nickers, the Hawcubites, and, in the day of Swift, Gay, and even of Johnson, the Mohocks, who made night hideous and the streets a terror, defying and often persistently ill-using the watch—amusements in which an imitation was successfully attempted in the present generation by the Corinthians and men about town who survived the Regency, but were defeated by the organisation of the "New Police," and the disappearance of the "Charlies," who were so frequently found screwed up in their watch boxes while the depredators committed all the mischief that their ingenuity could devise. In the last year of the reign of Charles II. a bold innovator, named Edward Heming, obtained a patent giving him the exclusive right to *light* the streets by placing a lamp before every tenth door on *moonless* nights from Michaelmas to Lady Day, from six to twelve o'clock, and, small as the improvement may seem to us, it was of immense importance.

Perhaps the most complete change in the *occupation* of the inhabitants of streets adjacent to Ludgate Hill was to be found in Paternoster Row. "My wife and I went to Paternoster Row, and there we bought some green watered moyre for a morning waistcoat." So writes old gossipy Pepys in his diary on November 21st, 1660.

For Paternoster Row was not at that time devoted to publishing and bookselling. It was the head-quarters of silk-mercers and lacemen till the Fire drove the more fashionable traders in these goods westward, and then "the Row" was a place for milliners and "tire-women" for a short time, till the booksellers took it. Before the Fire the stationers were mostly in the churchyard itself, in the "string," or straight side,* where the Chapter-house then stood, and its successor still stands. As each stationer had his sign, the list of houses reads like that of a row of taverns. It was at the White Greyhound that John Harrison first published Shakespeare's poems; at the Flower de Luce and the Crown

* The two sides of St. Paul's Churchyard were formerly known as the "bow" and the "string"; the south side having the form of a *bow* and the north side that of its rather slack *string*.

LUDGATE HILL AFTER THE REMOVAL OF LUD GATE—1780.

appeared the first edition of the *Merry Wives of Windsor;* and the Green Dragon, the Fox and the Angel, the Spread Eagle, the Gun and the Red Bull, are all associated with the publication of plays of the great dramatist.

The booksellers had suffered almost irreparable loss by the Great Fire, for a vast number of the volumes had been deposited in the crypt or church of St. Faith, beneath the cathedral, for safety, but the heat of the conflagration burnt them, and the whole were destroyed, to the value of £200,000. From that time, however, the trade was more than ever identified with this neighbourhood, and in what has been called "the Augustan age" of literature, when Addison, Steele, Pope, Swift, Prior, and the rest of the bigwigs whose names have come down to us in verse or prose, in *Spectators*, *Tatlers*, essays, poems, allegories, epigrams, odes, and choice latinity, the association of "the Row" and the publishers was inseparable, and a new era had opened for Ludgate Hill, which may be said to have continued to the present generation.

THE LUDGATE OF QUEEN ANNE AND THE GEORGES.

The "bloodless revolution" which had dethroned the second James had passed; the fear that once again high mass might be heard in London churches had given place to a rather rampant and self-assertive Protestantism, which was as militant as it was triumphant. Every Fifth of November the Pope was burnt in effigy, with much tumult, at Temple Bar, the turbulent procession going down Ludgate with drum and trumpet and flaming torches to light the bonfire; and though the Jacobites were never absent from London, and sometimes grew bold, and were always plotting, in spite of pillory and prison, "the Pretender" came to be as unlikely to gain authority as the Pope himself. For after the Peace of Ryswick, whereon there was a great and gorgeous Royal procession, in which William III. went from Greenwich through the City to Whitehall, the streets being lined by the trained bands, and the balconies and windows so hung with rich draperies and Turkey and Persian carpets that there had been nothing like it since the time of Elizabeth, the army was disbanded, and the disaffected plotters came to London, and there made themselves so busy that a proclamation had to be issued forbidding them to live within ten miles of the City, suppressing mass-houses and Popish schools, and empowering the seizure of arms found in the possession of Papists.

All this time, amidst wars, persecutions, revolution, dismay, recovery, and change of dynasty, the work of building the great cathedral had gone on, and it was in thanksgiving for the Peace of Ryswick that the first service was performed in it, December 2nd, 1697. The first stone was laid in June 1675, and the last in 1710. But on November 12th, 1702, Queen Anne, who had but just been crowned, went in state to the new cathedral with both Houses of Parliament, to return thanks for Marlborough's victories in the Low Countries, and for the success of Sir George Rooke at Vigo. And in 1704 and 1706 the great conqueror Marlborough himself marches triumphant, with a goodly company, up Ludgate Hill, to be entertained at the Guildhall, where the colours taken at Ramilies are hung by order of the Queen, while those that were among the spoils of honour at Blenheim are put up in the Hall at Westminster. Again in the latter year there is a solemn royal procession to the Cathedral, for the union of England and Scotland has been ratified and confirmed by Act of Parliament, and there is sober rejoicing thereat. A year before St. Paul's was finished the famous sermon denouncing and ridiculing the Whigs, and upholding passive obedience and submission to regal authority, was preached there before the Lord Mayor and Corporation by Dr. Sacheverel, the chaplain of St. Saviour, Southwark; and the effect of this and another similar discourse which he had already delivered at Derby was first to provoke the House of Commons to pronounce him guilty of malicious, scandalous, and seditious libels, and, secondly, to bring him to trial, and thereby to cause a riot among the common people, who thought that this was a device of the Presbyterians and Dissenters to overthrow, not Dr. Sacheverel only, but the Church of England. To prove at once their piety and their consistency, they escorted the Doctor from the Court to his lodgings in the Temple, and then went to the Presbyterian meeting-house of Mr. Burgess in New Court, gutted the building, carried doors, casements, and pews to Lincoln's Inn Fields, where they made them into a pile, with the pulpit on the top, and soon sent a select party to drag Burgess out of his house that they might put him in the pulpit to be burnt. Fortunately he had escaped by a back window, and the mob then directed their energies to destroying the meeting-house in Carter Lane, Blackfriars, and other Nonconformist chapels in the neighbourhood. The military and train bands were called out; drums were beating on Ludgate Hill as the troops marched to Blackfriars. The mob after some time was finally dispersed, and the Doctor who had caused the riot was inhibited from preaching for three years, his sermons being burnt at the Exchange by the common hangman. But when his term was out, the Queen, who probably relished his doctrine, and had no great love left for the Whigs, or for her once dear ally, Sarah, the Duchess of Marlborough, gave him the living of St. Andrew's, Holborn.

In 1710 the great Cathedral was finished—finished with what anxiety, pain, and sense of ill-treatment to the courageous, patient enthusiast who was its architect, few could tell; for he not only had to abandon much that was noble in his main design, but to alter at the caprice of the stupid bigot who succeeded Charles. Against the contradictory orders and opposition of Court and clergy he had to conciliate and to compromise, and but for the strenuous personal efforts he made he would have been overthrown by inferior workmen, who, after all, did not worthily carry out his great design. All the time that it was building, too, he received only the pittance of a common artificer, £200 a year; and even for half of this he had to wait till the whole building was completed.

We need not enter into any description of this vast and splendid structure, for those who visit it will easily obtain a guide to all its various attractions, its monuments, and its memorials. It is enough now to look up to its stupendous dome, to enter its still and solemn portals, and after we have gazed and dreamed and wondered, or, if it be during Divine service, have listened with devout hearts, and sung and prayed, to look at the epitaph which Mylne, the architect of Blackfriars Bridge, caused to be brought from the vaults beneath the church, and placed in gold letters over the Choir,—

"Subtus conditur,
Hujus ecclesiæ et urbis conditor,
Ch. Wren,
Qui vixit annos ultra nonaginta
Non sibi sed bono publico,
Lector. Si monumentum requiris,
Circumspice."

Yes, the Church was finished at a cost of £747,954 2s. 9d., paid for by a tax on coal brought into London. The statue of the Queen was placed in the midst of the western area, with the figures of Britain, France, Ireland, and America round the base of the pedestal. Bird was the sculptor, who also executed the figures in the "Conversion of St. Paul" on the entablature, and the statues of St. Paul, St. Peter, and St. James, on the pediment. The statue of Anne is a poor affair, and not more noticeable now than it was in the place it formerly occupied. Defoe wrote in 1722 that it was "very masterly done," though he could not say it was extremely like Her Majesty. There were some coarse and scurrilous verses which were made at the time, referring to the pretended liking of the Queen for *aqua vitæ*, and to the position of the statue with its back to the Church and facing a brandy-shop, which occupied a corner of the Churchyard; but the character of Anne, and the position she had to maintain, amidst much personal sorrow, and a strife in which she held a true and faithful part to the nation, have long ago confuted calumnies, and given her a place of honour in the national regard.

These and the succeeding years were again palmy days for the shops on Ludgate Hill and the booksellers in Paternoster Row, where, in 1710, Rivingtons, the Church publishers, lived at the Bible and Crown, and afterwards continued "Dodsley's Annual Register," with Edmund Burke as a contributor. At No 47 (afterwards the house of Messrs. W. & R. Chambers), Robert Baldwin published the *London Magazine*, commenced in 1732; and at the Ship and Black Swan were the progenitors of the Longmans, whose dinners and parties to authors and artists

THE BRISTOL COACH IN THE OUTER YARD OF THE BELL SAVAGE.

were once famous for the number of eminent men who were the guests.

The principal resort of booksellers and authors who had business together was the Chapter Coffee House, so often alluded to by poor Chatterton in his letters. This, like other houses of the kind, has changed its position since that time, and is indeed a tavern adapted to modern requirements, as publishers and authors now seldom transact business in the old fashion, and the ancient taverns about St. Paul's Churchyard having mostly disappeared. They had distinguished visitors in the days of the Georges, however,—the days of Pope, Swift, and afterwards of Doctor Johnson, Goldsmith, and Richardson, and those of Cowper, Darwin, Doctor Aikin, Mrs. Barbauld, Godwin, and other shining lights of the literary revival of the beginning of this century, who used to meet at the house of Johnson, the bookseller, where the premises of Messrs. Hitchcock now stand, and there dine with their genial host. Bonnycastle, the arithmetician, was there too, perhaps as the successor in the Yard to Cocker. The supremacy of the Church was to be found in the ancient days in Creed Lane, Ave Maria Lane, Canon Alley, Paternoster Row, and Amen Corner, the residence of the clergy of the Chapter House. We will say nothing of Do-Little Lane, which was probably named after some learned prebend; while Addle Lane is a corruption of Athelstan, the Saxon King, who had a palace there; and Sermon Lane has been disputed in favour of "Sheremoney," because Old Change, Cheapside, was the "old original" Mint of the Edwards, and in the lane close by were the shearers or clippers of the round pieces of metal, who thus prepared the coin for stamping after it had come from the "Blackloft" (in the same lane), where the silver was melted.

One of the most interesting of all the booksellers' shops, however, was that of Mr. Newbery, the publisher of children's books, at the very corner of St. Paul's Churchyard and Ludgate Street, now occupied by Messrs. Griffith and Farran, who maintain the juvenile reputation of the old house. Here was issued the original "Goody-Two-Shoes," "Valentine and Orson," and all the stories that, with their staring queer woodcuts and gilded covers, used to delight the hearts of our great-grandfathers when they were only just breeched and had a crown-piece to spend on Ludgate Hill.

There must have been rare company in the taverns and inns about Ludgate Hill in the early days of the Georges, and, doubtless, the Old Bell Savage had its share of it, even after Addison had written about it in the *Spectator*, and when the flying coaches, going for the whole journey at an average of five miles an hour, had come to be recognised as the consummation of the art of travelling, and when the mails went out regularly in coaches of their own. Steele and his jovial companions in the City have probably had many a bowl of punch and tobacco at Dolly's or elsewhere, for smoking had been long established as a common practice, and there were tobacco houses to which country squires and men about town went to have, as it were, a smoking debauch, coming out dazed and drunk, and only recovered by coffee and wet cloths round their temples, as those who list may read in that curious but not always edifying book, "The London Spy," by Ned Ward. There were alehouses and ordinaries enough all about this neighbourhood to suit any purse, and we find Swift in his Journal to Stella saying, "To-day I was all about St. Paul's, and up at the top like a fool, with Sir Andrew Fountain and two more; and spent seven shillings for my dinner like a puppy. This is the second time he has served me so; but I will never do it again, though all mankind should persuade me—unconsidering puppies." Such is the fretful intimation in one of those saddest of epistles, Swift's letters to Stella, wherein we see the gloomy, carping temper of the man, who was, even then, approaching the dark and melancholy end of his turbulent disputes. To go to the top of St. Paul's and pay for his own dinner afterwards, instead of being treated, as he had hoped and might reasonably have expected, when he could ill afford more than a shilling ordinary! There is no record of the spectacle from the golden ball, and yet Swift might have written a great satire on the subject.

There was one man who, perhaps more than poet, essayist, or even dramatist, preserved for us the true picture of what London was in the early Georgian period; and he was one of the constant visitors to Ludgate Hill and all its neighbourhood, for he was an engraver to the booksellers in his youth, had marked with observant eye, and soon represented with unerring, and, at the same time, unflattering pencil, the aspect of the streets. His name was William Hogarth, and from his pictures we learn more of Bridewell, of the narrow lanes and alleys, of the bustle of the markets, the excesses of the mob, the crime and jollity and extravagance and drollery of London life, than from most written descriptions—for from a highwayman on the way to execution from Newgate, to the progress of the civic carriage in the Lord Mayor's Show, he had seen and estimated them all. And, speaking of Lord Mayor's Shows, these had come to be the only pageants left to the populace by the time that the succession was fixed. The old allegorical structures that occupied the streets during a royal progress had already become historical, coaches of state were comparatively common, all gold and varnish and great heraldic panels, and full of carved devices. A few of these, a troop of Life Guards, a dozen heralding trumpeters, and a score of banners, with the attendant footmen and gentlemen-at-arms, made a royal procession. There were only the Lord Mayors' Shows left, and these were still stately affairs, especially as that part of the journey to Westminster was still made by water in the grand barges of the City Companies, before the Conservancy of the Thames was taken from the City. An account of the great civic shows that have wound their way round the bow of St. Paul's, and so come with a sudden rush of colour and sparkle of steel and gold and blare of music, down the hill to Fleet Bridge, would fill a volume. We need not go back to the earliest on record when, on the passage of Henry III. and Eleanor of Provence through London, they were escorted by the mayor, aldermen, and 350 mounted citizens apparelled in robes of embroidered silk, and each carrying in his hand a cup of gold or silver, in token of the claim of the Lord Mayor to act as Chief Butler at the Coronation; nor will we describe the grand water procession in honour of the coronation of Anne Boleyn, when the Mayor's barge, covered

with red cloth, was garnished with goodly banners and
streamers, and hung with emblazoned shields, while a band
of "shalms, shagbushes, and divers other instruments"
made good harmony, as the fifty barges of the City Companies, marshalled by three light wherries with officers,
followed, all gorgeously bedight; and before all went
another barge full of ordnance, containing a dragon vomiting
wild fire, and surrounding it terrible monsters and savages
also vomiting fire, discharging squibs, and making hideous
noises. Flags of silk, and sails of cloth of gold and silver,
banners with devices and shields of beaten gold, were the
decorations of the Lord Mayor's barge, and there was also
a floating pageant of a white falcon on a rock environed with
white and red roses, the cognisance of the House of
Boleyn.

There have been some not very intelligible or successful
attempts to revive the old civic pageants even in our own
time, but the last example of the truly gorgeous shows
of the Middle Ages was that of John Leman, of the Fishmongers' Company, who was Mayor in the reign of James I.
The pageant was designed by Munday, one of the Shakespearean dramatists, and the drawings, now in possession
of the Fishmongers' Company, are full of fancy. The first
pageant represented a buss, or Dutch fishing-boat, on wheels.
The fishermen in it were busy drawing up nets full of live
fish, and throwing them to the people. On the mast and at
the head of the boat were the insignia of the company—
St. Peter's keys and two arms supporting a crown. The
second pageant was a gigantic crowned dolphin, ridden
by Arion. The third pageant was the King of the Moors,
riding on a golden leopard, and scattering gold and silver
freely around him. He was attended by six tributary kings
in gilt armour on horseback, each carrying a dart and gold
and silver ingots. This pageant was in honour of the Fishmongers' brethren, the Goldsmiths. The fourth pageant
was the usual pictorial pun on the Lord Mayor's name and
crest. The car bore a large lemon-tree full of golden fruit,
with a pelican in her nest feeding her young (proper). At
the top of the tree sat five children, representing the five
senses. The boys were dressed as women, each with her

A LORD MAYOR'S SHOW (*from Hogarth*).

emblem—Seeing, by an eagle; Hearing, by a hart; Touch, by a spider; Tasting, by an ape; and Smelling, by a dog. The fifth pageant was Sir William Walworth's bower, which was hung with the shields of all Lord Mayors who had been Fishmongers. Upon a tomb within the bower was laid the effigy in knightly armour of Sir William, the slayer of Wat Tyler. Five mounted knights attended the car, and a mounted man-at-arms bore Wat Tyler's head upon a dagger. In attendance were six trumpeters and twenty-four halberdiers, arrayed in light blue silk, emblazoned with the Fishmongers' arms on the breast and Walworth's on the back. Then followed an angel with golden wings and crown, riding on horseback, who, on the Lord Mayor's approach, with a golden rod awoke Sir William from his long sleep, and the two then became speakers in the interlude. The great central pageant was a triumphal car drawn by two mermen and two mermaids. In the highest place sat a guardian angel defending the crown of Richard II., who sat just below her. Under the King sat female personifications of the royal virtues, Truth, Virtue, Honour, Temperance, Fortitude, Zeal, Equity, Conscience, beating down Treason and Mutiny, the two last being enacted "by burly men." In a seat corresponding with the King's sat Justice, and below her Authority, Law, Vigilance, Peace, Plenty, and Discipline.

This was the grandest show that was to be seen on Ludgate Hill for many a day, and the less political and, indeed, very commonplace displays of the Georges fall far below it. After the coronation of George III., however, when their Majesties went to the civic dinner, Ludgate Hill and the other streets on the route made a pageant which was, in its way, very grand and impressive. Sir Samuel Fludyer was Lord Mayor then (in 1761), and the Thames was covered with boats and gilded barges, with strange allegorical figures in quaint dresses in some of them. The Lord Mayor landed on the return journey at the Temple, and there his pageant waited till the royal procession had gone on some time. Every house from Temple Bar to Guildhall was crowded from top to bottom, and all the citizens kept open house for their friends. The royal family stopped at the house of Mr. Barclay, the Quaker, where from the balcony, hung with crimson silk damask, they saw the civic pageant go by, and then followed to the feast at Guildhall. But just before the pageant arrived came Mr. Pitt in his chariot, accompanied by Earl Temple; and the great commoner had the real honour, for at every step the mob clung about every part of the vehicle, hung upon the wheels, hugged his footmen, and even kissed his horses. It was a rough time, the successor of still rougher times, when an enthusiastic mob would not be denied, and it required some nerve to face the imminent danger of popularity.

Wilkes must have found it so, for he ran the gauntlet both of favour and disfavour when his trial was proceeding, after the obnoxious number of the *North Briton* had been issued from Ludgate Hill; and a later date, when, on his being arrested, the populace unhorsed the coach, turned out the tipstaves, who would probably have been killed but for Wilkes' entreaties, and drew the popular representative of Middlesex up Ludgate Hill and as far as Spitalfields.

The Fleet, Fleet Marriages, the Market, the Prisons, Blackfriars Bridge.

Even to those of us who have heard of "runaway matches" and marriages at Gretna Green, on the borders between England and Scotland (where it used to be pretended, but without much authenticity, that the ceremony was performed by a blacksmith)—the Fleet marriages are now scarcely credible. There is ample evidence, however, that within the Fleet or its liberties—in dingy lodgings, low taverns or beerhouses—a number of besotted, broken-down, and unscrupulous parsons, drunken chaplains, and other debased clergymen carried on a competitive business in marrying people with little or no ceremony. Some of those weddings were originally performed in the chapel of the prison; but the business became so extensive that they were afterwards celebrated in some dingy room in one or other of the taverns, each of which kept its book of registers. These marriages were not, of course, strictly legal, and yet in such a condition was the ecclesiastical law that they were tacitly recognised as being valid, and if conducted by one of the Fleet parsons were not to be dissolved. A collection of the registrar books, weighing more than a ton, and recording Fleet marriages between 1686 and 1754 were purchased by the Government in 1821, and deposited in the registry office of the Bishop of London in Doctors' Commons, and among the names are many of great celebrity and high rank.

There were three classes of marriages at the Fleet—those of couples who had eloped and desired to be married immediately and secretly; those who followed a kind of fashion (for it became fashionable with a certain "fast" set of people to be married at the Fleet), or who, having made up their minds in a moment, hurried to the parson before they had time to change it; and those in which women were inveigled under some false pretence, or forcibly carried there, and intimidated into consenting to a ceremony of which they did not understand the meaning, but which by a few incoherent words bound them to a life-long compact. The parsons had touts about Ludgate Hill and Fleet Market, or themselves stood at their doors inviting likely couples to come in and be married; and it may be imagined what were the scandalous results of such a disgraceful practice. A bride or a bridegroom could be found at a few minutes' notice for a consideration, and registers could either be destroyed or ante-dated if a suitable arrangement were made. It was known that extravagant ladies had been to the Fleet, and had hired husbands for the ceremony, merely that they might obtain a certificate enabling them to evade their creditors by pleading coverture against any action for debt.

"Marriages, with a license certificate and a crown stamp, *at a guinea*, at the new chapel, next door to the china shop, near Fleet Bridge, by a regular-bred clergyman, and not by a Fleet parson" . . . is part of an advertisement in the *Daily Advertiser* in 1749; and a handbill of the period invites candidates for matrimony to "the true chapel at the Old Red Hand and Mitre, three doors from Fleet Lane, and next door to the White Swan," where the ceremony was performed "by authority, by the Reverend Mr. Symson, educated at the University of Cambridge, and late Chaplain to the Earl of Rothes." An emphatic line at the foot of the bill is, "N.B. Without imposition." One window bears a board, with "Weddings performed cheap here"; another announces "The old and true Register"; and at the Horseshoe and Magpie, the Rainbow Coffee-house at the corner of the Ditch, the Hand and Pen, the Bishop Blaize, the Fighting Cocks, the Naked Boy, and other brandy-shops, taverns, and ale-houses, some of them kept by the turnkeys, and most of them houses of call for the parsons, who are called in by the landlord, and share their fees with him, the nefarious work goes on daily. Besides the numbers who are married by force or guile, and those who are now and then kidnapped and robbed by being frightened out of the fees before they are permitted to escape, scores of people go through the Fleet ceremony in preference to that of the regular celebration at church, and parties of half-intoxicated sailors and their lasses from Wapping, or of other roysterers with their partners, have been known to go to be married as a kind of termination to a frolic. The same kind of marriages were also held at Mayfair, where a rascally clergyman named Keith, famous in those days, had a chapel, and, as Horace Walpole said, made "a very bishopric of revenue." This fellow was excommunicated, but he retorted by excommunicating at his own chapel the bishop, the judge of the Ecclesiastical Court, and two reverend doctors. He was imprisoned in the Fleet, but left curates in charge of his Mayfair business, and commenced another in the prison. When it was threatened that the bishops would put an end to these illegal marriages, Keith swore he would raise money to buy a plot of ground for a cemetery, and "under-bury" them. The Fleet and Mayfair marriages were a public scandal, but the latter especially were supported by the aristocracy. It was in Mayfair that the Duke of Hamilton, who was impatient to marry one of the beautiful Miss Gunnings, had the marriage ceremony performed at the chapel at half-past twelve at night. Keith died in the Fleet prison in 1758, four years after the Act against clandestine marriages came into operation. The people of rank were becoming a little alarmed at the fashion of the Fleet, but the mischief had become so great that the business increased

FLEET PARSONS AND FLEET MARRIAGES.

during the few months' interval between the passing of the Act and its operation, and therefore before the law came in force 217 marriages were entered there in one register, and 61 marriages were performed at Mayfair, so eager were couples to make the most of the interval, and so much had the evil custom prevailed.

Fleet Market, which was established when the Fleet Ditch had been covered in from the corner of the foot of Ludgate to Holborn Bridge, was instituted when the site of Stocks' Market, at the corner of the Poultry, was wanted for the building of the Mansion House in 1738, the year in which two large birds, said to be eagles or cormorants, were seen perched one on the cross, and the other on the pineapple on St. Paul's. All sorts of superstitious notions got about, and the appearance was said to be ominous. Very likely it was, for the naval authorities, seeing what crowds assembled on Ludgate Hill, took advantage of public curiosity by securing a live turkey to the top of the monument on Fish Street Hill, and when a large number of people had gone to stare at it the press-gangs made a raid and kidnapped a number of likely young fellows to be taken to serve on board His Majesty's fleet. The prisons of Bridewell, the Fleet, Newgate, and even that of Ludgate, were still in full operation, and the whole neighbourhood about the Fleet Valley, and indeed from Temple Bar to the Old Bailey, and from Bridewell to Saffron Hill, teemed with the haunts of vice and crime. There were houses which were dens of murderers, coiners, and thieves, and some of them communicated by cellars and secret passages, so that victims who were decoyed into them could be made away with, and the bodies of missing men were more than once discovered in vaults and dark passages. It seemed as though the great prison of Newgate, which, like the Fleet and Bridewell, had been rebuilt after the Fire, attracted the gaol-birds, by an evil fascination, to hover around its precincts, and to roost in the tangle of courts and alleys about the banks of the foul stream which flowed in the Holborn Valley at the foot of Ludgate Hill. When Fielding wrote that strange, repulsive history of Jonathan Wild, the trade of the thief-taker and the thief was one, for the thief-taker was often the decoy, and himself had graduated in crime that he might afterwards live on the "blood money" gained by informing on his victims, who had once been his confederates. Not only was the Fleet Ditch, before it was

THE LAST OF FLEET DITCH.

enclosed, dangerous to passengers, who at night often fell into the black stream and were drowned, but it was the dark scene of midnight murders perpetrated in the impenetrable jungle of decaying and ruinous houses that stood on the space on the Fleet Street side towards St. Andrew's Church.

The Newgate Calendar—the true Newgate Calendar—the records and reports of the Ordinaries of Newgate, alone could give any idea of the horrors of that dreadful prison in a time when the press-yard was still in use as a place of torture to extract confessions, or even in the later time when highwaymen, manacled but defiant, sat together in one of the great rooms of the gaol, and there caroused or crouched silent and moody till they were taken out and went the road to Tyburn; of murderers in the condemned cells, and of unfortunate prisoners wrongly condemned to suffer death for crimes that they had not committed, in the days when hanging was the short and easy method of punishment, even for petty larceny, and yet when crime was rampant and murder scarcely seemed to be diminished by the sight of the gallows. There were no executions at Newgate then—Tyburn was the place where felons were executed—except in cases when they were hanged in front of the places where the offence for which they suffered had been committed; and in the exceptions made for piracy, when the bodies of the malefactors swung in chains at Execution Dock. It was not till 1783 that the place of execution was changed from Tyburn to the front of Newgate, and at that period the mode of hanging was to take the prisoner beneath the gibbet in a cart, which was driven from under him when the fatal knot had been fastened and the cap drawn over his eyes. The gallows was built with three cross-beams, that three rows of prisoners might be executed at one time; an awful indication of the wholesale infliction of capital punishment which characterised the times. In 1785 the "new drop" was substituted for the cart, and the sufferers were no longer "turned off"; but hanging became a fine art—and "Ketch" was succeeded by the predecessors of Marwood. Between February and December that year ninety-six persons suffered the penalty of death at Newgate, and in the following year the last instance took place of burning the body by heaping faggots round and over it—as it hung upon a low gibbet—and setting them on fire. It was the corpse of a woman that closed the list of those which had been subjected to this dreadful cremation. But both before and after executions took place at Newgate, Surgeons' Hall received the bodies of the criminals from the gallows. Here, in 1760, the corpse of Lord Ferrers was brought from Tyburn for the completion of the sentence by disembowelling, and here it was exposed to view. Near Surgeons' Hall, at No. 12, Green Arbour Court, at the corner of Breakneck Steps, in Seacole Lane, lodged Oliver Goldsmith from 1758 to 1760. It was here he was writing his "Polite Learning Enquiry" when Dr. Percy called on him and found him in great poverty. At the bottom of Breakneck Steps, when the place existed at a much later date, might still be seen a massy fragment of the old city wall, which was near the Ballium, or outer bail. Seacole Lane was opposite the entrance to the Old Bailey from St. Martin's Court, Ludgate Hill. The present Central Criminal Court, established in 1834, forms part of the Sessions House, divided by a broad paved yard from the prison. Here every kind of offence is tried, and the journey is a short one from "dock" to "cell." The site of Surgeons' Hall was taken into that of the old Justice Hall, and the Sessions House and Court House were built on it in 1809. Even to-day any one who visits the entirely re-modelled prison, or sits and listens to the trials in the Sessions House, may fancy that he sees some of the remnants that have been bequeathed to us from the evil times when, every Monday, the front of the gaol showed a horrible spectacle, which was supposed to be in the interests of humanity; and even the thoughts of the stately dining-room above the Old Court, where, during the Old Bailey sittings, the sheriffs' dinners are served, at which judges and civic officials and pleaders sit down daily, remind us of the line that marks the carelessness of justice and the hurried hearing of evidence and pronouncing sentence in the days when it was said—

"Wretches hang that jurymen may dine."

There are many of us who remember, not without a shudder, the hanging days at the Old Bailey, and how, with a sickening sense, we have hurried past just as the turbulent, hoarse, and brutal crowd came pouring into Ludgate Hill, or went their way towards Smithfield, when the show was over, and the rigid corpse had ceased to swing, and was "cut down."

It seems horrible to think of even now, and yet it was no longer ago than 1864 that the seven pirates were hanged there for murder on the high seas. It is a shorter time since the gallows and its dreadful burden was taken inside the gaol, so that sensitive people could go, even on a Monday, down the Old Bailey. The aspect of the place has changed since then. Williams's famous boiled beef shop, which used to be so crowded after an execution morning, has disappeared. We should all be shocked to hear that a prisoner was to be hanged in public again, and yet it is held by some that the very fact of our shirking the sight and hiding the deed is an argument in favour of abolishing the gallows altogether. We leave that argument, for it is not within the scope of these memorials; but how far we seem to have got from the times of Jack Sheppard, the " good old times " when prisoners were hung in batches—the murderer, the highwayman, the unfortunate woman who has pilfered that she might not starve; the lad guilty of petty larceny, who had to stand on a stool because he was too small for the rope to reach him! These were the times when the prison had its revenge even on the Court, and when the rue strewn in front of the dock and the bench could not avert the gaol-fever that crept from the loathsome cells into the court itself, and struck down judge and counsel and officers. How far we are even from the days when my Lord Tomnoddy "jumped up at the news," exclaiming,—

> "Ropedancers a score
> I've seen before—
> Madame Sacchi, Antonio, and Master Blackmore;
> But to see a man swing
> At the end of a string,
> With his neck in a noose, will be quite a new thing."

When Barham (Ingoldsby), canon of St. Paul's, wrote his satire in the house of the clergy in the churchyard, every window at the tavern, and other houses opposite Newgate Prison, was let at a high price on hanging mornings, and from early dawn a ruffianly mob pushed, and swore, and yelled, and hooted below; hooted at authority, hooted at respectability, cursed at remonstrance, yelled the wretched being who was the centre of attraction out of the world, and fought and robbed, and sometimes nearly murdered under the very gallows itself.

The old Prison of Ludgate was pulled down when the old gates of the City were removed on the accession of George III. in 1760, and however much the ancient structure of the gate itself may have been regretted, the way was opened clear and free from the foot of the hill to St. Paul's. The very walls of the wretched prison might have echoed the sighs of the wretches who had been incarcerated there, and there were sermons in the stones, but they were all carted away and sold as building materials for £148. The statue of Elizabeth was placed in a niche of the outer wall of St. Dunstan's Church, Fleet Street, where it remains. The figures of the family of Lud were presented to Sir Francis Gosling, who meant to re-erect them at the east end of the same church, but somehow they were stowed away in the parish bone-house, where they remained till the Marquis of Hertford bought them, and along with the old St. Dunstan's clock and its two giants, that struck the hour on a bell, took them to his villa at Regent's Park. The few "poor debtors" who were at Ludgate were removed to the London Workhouse in Bishopsgate Street, where it is to be hoped they fared better than by the begging-box and the doles of their old gaol.

The Fleet, however, was full of prisoners. It had been rebuilt after the Fire, and the old prison, which had once been the scene of the Court of the Star Chamber, was changed. There were no State prisoners, but it was still the abode of misery and cruelty, and the poor debtors, victims of rapacious or indifferent governors and gaolers, were loaded with irons, placed to sleep in damp cellars, starved, unclothed, and to judge from the revelations that were made, often tortured by wooden manacles, shaped like tailors' sleeve-boards, the broad end having a hole for the neck, and the narrow end one for the right hand, which had to be constantly raised; a shocking punishment, not excelled by boot and screw. Bridewell, too, had been rebuilt after the burning, and was now a place of reformation (?) and punishment for persons of bad character, who were set to beat oakum, and were whipped on the bare shoulders, while the governor sat and looked on, till he gave the signal by knocking with a hammer after a certain number of lashes had been inflicted. Bridewell was the Court of Government for Bethlehem Hospital, which in 1829 had its house of occupation, or, as we should call it, a reformatory industrial school; but Bridewell had an industrial school of its own, as well as being a house of correction for idle apprentices. The Bridewell boys, who were apprenticed to masters of various trades in the building, which was a hospital or *workhouse* for indigent persons, wore a kind of livery, and were mostly to be seen at fires, where they were very active in working an engine belonging to the hospital; but they were a disorderly, noisy set of fellows, and added considerably to the discomforts of the passengers about Ludgate Hill. It became a prison for thieves and misdemeanants till 1863, when a portion of the prison was taken down, and committals of criminals and the worst misdemeanants were made to the City Prison at Holloway. The committal of unruly and disobedient City apprentices to Bridewell by the Chamberlain of London, who has about 3,000 of these youths under his jurisdiction, is still maintained. The court-house and hall were handsome, and the latter was adorned with some good portraits of the successive presidents, and a full-length of Charles II. by Sir Peter Lely, a cartoon of the Good Samaritan by Dadds, and a large picture of Edward VI. transferring the hospital to the City of London. Little more than the offices remained after the building was demolished.

But we must remember that Newgate, Bridewell, and the Fleet were all rebuilt after 1780, when they were burned down in the anti-Popery riots and the prisoners released. Of that dreadful time the most graphic and intensely interesting account of the scene about Ludgate Hill, before Newgate, and in the adjacent portion of Holborn, is familiar to most readers in the pages of "Barnaby Rudge." To transcribe the story, as told by the great novelist, would occupy too much space, and after that marvellous account it would be folly to attempt another that could approach it for general accuracy, or for picturesque effect. Of what the Fleet Prison was when it was devoted only to the reception of debtors, the same master-hand has given a faithful and pathetic narrative in the famous "Pickwick Papers," and to them also we surely need scarcely refer our readers.

Fleet Prison was on the east side of the Market—a large, long brick building, shut in by surrounding houses and high walls, and with galleries in every story leading from one end of the house to the other, with the rooms for the prisoners on each side. In order to understand what the Fleet Prison was really like it is necessary to read between the lines of the reports that were from time to time made upon it before it was finally pulled down. Probably the most authentic *official* statement is to be found in the evidence of Mr. Nicholas Nixon, himself the deputy and sole acting warden ; from this we learn that the only other officers beside the deputy-warden and his clerk were three turnkeys, one watchman, and one scavenger. The turnkeys were paid a guinea a week each, and had each a room, which they partitioned off and occasionally let to prisoners. The watchman was also the acting scavenger, and the crier to the prison, and, being himself a prisoner, received 10s. 6d. a week and a free lodging, as well as some emoluments for bringing down prisoners to inquirers, and for lighting the lamps in the galleries. Thefts were common in the prison, and it was the duty of the crier to "cry" the stolen articles. There was one crier who was himself the thief, purloining portable property that he might cry it and obtain the reward for its recovery.

All manner of provisions were brought into the prison and sold as they might be in the streets, but only with the authority of the warden and his deputy, and beer and ale sold at the tap was on the credit of the deputy. There was recently no licence for selling wine, and spirituous liquors were prohibited. The cook and the racket-master, being officers of the prisoners, were elected by them twice a year. Only prisoners who paid their entrance fees were entitled to admission to rooms in the prison on the *master's* side, where they had a priority to chummage, or being placed to share a room with others, according to rotation on their seniority as prisoners. A few venerable prisoners were exempt from having newer arrivals *chummed* upon them, or sent to share their rooms. No fees were paid on the *common* side, which was devoted to the unfortunate prisoners who swore they were not worth five pounds in the world, and were allowed to participate in the subscriptions collected from passers-by at the begging-grate, where each of the entitled prisoners stood to ask for alms, each in rotation, for twenty-four hours. Besides the begging-grate, there were sometimes charitable donations distributed among the very poorest prisoners, and £500 a year, granted for the purpose by Act of Parliament, was distributed amongst the poor prisoners indiscriminately. Some of these unfortunate wretches waited on the wealthy ones, and so added a little to the miserable pittance which of itself would seldom keep them from starvation. The racket-masters earned a guinea a week each, as they were paid by the game. Fifteen-pence a week was the rent of a lodging on the master's side. Lights and fires had to be extinguished in the coffee-room and tap at eleven o'clock, before which all strangers were expected to leave the building; but this was not always complied with, and scenes of riot and disorder were frequent, while the morals of the place were represented by a small and almost unknown quantity. There appears to have been constant neglect, misery, confusion, and disorder. Two clubs were established, one in the coffee-room and another in the tap-room, to which strangers were admitted. The chapel was very badly attended, though the prison gates were kept locked during the time of service. At other times the key was turned, on the average, about once a minute. The prison was "nearly" secured against fire, all the rooms except the top flight being arched with brick. No official medical attendance was provided. Four times a year an officer of the Court of Common Pleas went to look at the prison, before each term, and it was whitewashed as often as that operation was thought to be necessary, and repaired about once in three years. There were about 300 prisoners in the building and the *rules*, which extended to a portion of the neighbourhood, to about the circumference of three-quarters of a mile, where prisoners might be entitled to take a lodging by giving sufficient security to the warden by an "instrument" upon a twenty-shilling stamp, and by paying an enquiry fee and percentage on the amount of the debt. These and other fees formed the rather handsome emoluments of the warden or his deputy; and there were also day rules to enable prisoners to be out during term-time every day the Court sat. The expense of a day rule was £2 7s. for the whole time, if the charge was under £500, and 4s. 6d. a day additional. Thus amidst squalor, misery, and vice, lived the prisoners in the Fleet and its rules, and many of them lived in a kind of coarse luxury and profusion, which was all the more striking because of the sickness and starvation to which the penniless sufferers on the poor side were condemned.

Fleet Market occupied the space now occupied by Farringdon Circus, and extended from the east end of Fleet Street to the bottom of Snow Hill. It really consisted of two rows of butchers' shops, a turret with a clock in the centre, and at the north end an open space with stalls for fish and vegetables.

In a later edition of the "Pickwick Papers" Mr. Charles Dickens, in noting that vast improvements had taken place since its first issue, was able to conclude with the triumphant words, "*and the Fleet Prison is pulled down*"—an event to which his admirable exposure of its abuses doubtless contributed. It was abolished in 1842, and the few inmates who then remained were drafted to the Queen's Bench. The site, comprising about an acre, was purchased of the Government by the Corporation of London for £25,000. In 1846 the prison was taken down, and the materials sold. The whole area both of the Fleet and of the nest of wretched houses demolished on the removal of the market to the new Farringdon Market lay for seventeen years a waste—a ruin of bricks, stones, and excavations, the resort of betting-men and touts, and the haunt of the London ruffian, who fought, gambled, and indulged in horse play until the commencement of the work for bridging the Holborn Valley with the new viaduct.

From the 19th of November, 1769, there had been a bridge across the Thames at Blackfriars, and the Fleet Bridge and that at Bridewell, as well as the one at Holborn, had become unnecessary and was removed. The first pile was driven in the middle of the Thames on the 7th of June, 1760, on the accession of George III. It was built by the Corporation, and a toll was charged to help to defray the cost of the bridge and the large improvements in the streets and approaches. The toll-houses were burnt by the "No Popery" rioters, and the money-boxes stolen; but the obnoxious tax of a halfpenny on week-days and a penny on Sundays continued. The architect whose design was chosen was Robert Mylne, a young Scotch engineer, poor and almost unknown, who had just come from Italy, where he had gained a prize. Smeaton, the great engineer, and Gwynn, the friend of Dr. Johnson, who had written a great work on London improvements, were competitors; but Mylne gained the commission, and at once got into hot water with the newspapers, where his opponents, and particularly Dr. Johnson, denounced the notion of building a bridge on elliptical instead of semi-circular arches. Time served to prove that they were right, for though Mylne built a beautiful bridge— was appointed Surveyor of St. Paul's Cathedral (where his tomb is beside that of Wren), and rebuilt Bridge Street, where he had a fine house, afterwards the York Hotel— Old Blackfriars Bridge did not stand, and cost a great deal in repairs before it was determined to take it down. Johnson afterwards became friendly with Mylne, and used to dine at his house. Mylne's success was attributed to his friends being supporters of the Bute Ministry. The great antagonist of that Administration, John Wilkes, had the place of honour opposite the bridge-foot at the end of Fleet Street, where an obelisk was erected to him as the representative of the ward of Farringdon Without, and to celebrate his struggle for political liberty, for which he was then in prison. It fared worse with the memory of Pitt, after whom the bridge was to be called, and to whom the tablet recording its completion inscribed the whole work as a memorial. The inscription and the whole business was ridiculed, and nothing would cause the name "Pitt" Bridge to stick. It became Blackfriars Bridge, and the references to the great Minister only remained on the tablet, and in Chatham Place, William Street, and Earl Street.

With the completion of the bridge a great improvement took place in the neighbourhood. The streets were still dark, lighted only by oil-lamps; but these were placed at more frequent intervals, and, dim as they were, gave some light, especially in open thoroughfares. The pavements were still defective, and in the byeways and side streets the mud and gutters were a common nuisance, and a serious danger, nor were robberies infrequent. Still, there was a great change since Johnson wrote,—

> "Prepare for death if here at night you roam,
> And sign your will before you sup from home;
> Some fiery fop, with new commission vain
> Who sleeps on brambles till he kills his man;
> Some frolic drunkard, reeling from a feast,
> Provokes a broil, and stabs you for a jest.
> Yet even these heroes, mischievously gay,
> Lords of the streets and terrors of the way,
> Flush'd as they are with folly, youth, and wine,
> Their prudent insults to the poor confine;
> Afar they mark the flambeau's light approach,
> And shun the shining train and golden coach."

What with these Hectors and the armed footpads who, in gangs, waylaid and robbed people even in the City, London was a dangerous place at night in the middle of the last century, and with the doubtful aid of the link-boys who professed to light belated passengers, for, as Gay tells us,—

> "Trust him not along the lonely wall;
> In the midway he'll quench the flaming brand,
> And share the booty with the pilf'ring band.
> Still keep the public streets, where oily rays,
> Shot from the crystal lamp, o'erspread thy ways."

The oily rays were to be extinguished in good time, however, in favour of the brighter illumination. The Paving and Lighting Act of 1762 did much, and the lamp-lighter became an important public character; but on the 28th of January, 1807, Winzer had illuminated Pall Mall with "coal-gas," and, in 1812, he had formed his company (the origin of the Gas Light and Coke Company), and London was resplendent.

Ludgate Hill in the New Light.

Blackfriars Bridge had been finished while England was at war with America and at war with France, in the midst of slack trade, want, and public disturbance; but yet the great thoroughfares were full of life and bustle, the shops were gay, and the business of the world went on. Ludgate Hill had had its shows and processions, one of which was pathetic, for it was on the occasion of the thanksgiving at St. Paul's for the recovery of the King from the attack of insanity from which he had been suffering. Their Majesties and the Royal Family went in state, with peers, judges, statesmen; and at Temple Bar the civic dignitaries mounted white palfreys, which were each decorated with three dozen "favours," blue and white. There were flags, guards of honour, and lacqueys sumptuously apparelled, in the midst of whom eight cream-coloured horses drew their Majesties in a coach, the panels and front of which were of glass instead of leather. By the Queen's special desire all the London "charity children" assembled in the galleries, in the place they usually occupied at their anniversary meeting, and the assembly was an imposing one, while the aspect of the streets, and the whole line of Ludgate Hill, was that of a city *en fête*. This was the most remarkable procession which the Hill had seen for some years; but there followed the funereal and yet superb *cortége* which accompanied the body of our great naval hero, Nelson, to the tomb, after the solemn procession which conveyed it from Greenwich to Whitehall. The vast and brilliant assembly beneath the dome of the Cathedral was illuminated by a lantern, or octagonal frame holding 200 patent lamps. The rejoicings for the jubilee of the reign of George III., and the continued festivities on the visit of the Allied Sovereigns after the defeat of Napoleon Bonaparte in 1814, may be said to close the list of truly magnificent spectacles, though in the latter so many people were killed or injured by the crowds which assembled without restraint or order that it was a mournful anniversary for some families. The sombre but impressive spectacle when the body of "the hero of a hundred fights"—the victor of Waterloo—was borne to St. Paul's will not be forgotten by those who stood on Ludgate Hill on the 18th of November, 1852.

LUDGATE HILL ON FEB. 27TH, 1872.

Another memorable scene was presented by Ludgate Hill on that happy occasion when, on the 27th of February,

1872, the recovery of the Prince of Wales from an illness which had caused long anxiety to the nation, was celebrated by a public thanksgiving day by the Queen, the Prince, and the whole of the Royal Family in England, at St. Paul's Cathedral.

I had the honour of assisting to organise a committee for forming a general plan of decorating Ludgate Hill; and the arrangement of flags, banners, and Venetian masts was acknowledged to be most effective, not the least striking feature of the show being displayed at the moment when the Royal procession commenced the ascent of the Hill, when the appearance of Her Majesty and the Prince was saluted by the sudden flutter of a multitude of small flags, which, at a given signal, waved simultaneously from all the windows.

All this time the Old Bell Savage had been sedately accommodating itself to the altered times, and from its outer yard—where houses had stood, and where, at No. 11, Grinling Gibbons, the famous wood-carver, had once lived, and, as Walpole tells us, had set up for a sign a pot of flowers so beautifully carved that they shook with the rumble of the carriages—the Bristol coach now ran, as well as other "high-flyers," and the old place was in a periodical bustle of excitement; while in its sedate coffee-room snug parties came to eat "a rump and dozen," or to sip some of the famous bees-wing port.

It was probably here that the story was told of the lady, the widow of a Mr. Rugg, who bestowed her hand and a large fortune on Wilkes' successor, Alderman Price, and, on being afterwards complimented on her re-marriage, said, "Yes, I have got rid of my old Rugg for a good Price"; and Wilkes' remark to a friend, when he had just entered his inn from the bear-garden, and a man, who spoke insultingly to him, had just been served with a "grill," was of the same kind, "Ah, the difference between this and the bear-garden is, that here they bring the steak to the bear, and there they take the bear to the stake."

There were some well-known characters to be seen in the famous old hostelry about that period during the Wilkes' disturbances, and what time his political successor, Mr. Waithman, the linendraper, had his shop over yonder at the corner of Bridge Street and Fleet Street. Waithman had the same honour as Wilkes, and his obelisk graced the

TIM-BUC-TOO.

bridge-foot not far from his shop. There are the two stone memorials still, but they have been shifted, Waithman's to Farringdon Street, while the other stands in the mouth of

PORTION OF OLD LONDON WALL NEAR THE "BARBICAN," DISCOVERED IN ST. MARTIN'S COURT, LUDGATE HILL.

Ludgate Circus, though few people know which is which. Alderman Waithman was a clear debater, a busy politician in the Common Council, and Cobbett, who disliked him, calls him the Cock of the Democratic Party. He had a talent for the stage, had acted Macbeth, and was uncle to the famous John Reeve, the low comedian. He was elected for the ward of Farringdon in 1796, and went to Parliament as member for the City in 1818, when he defeated Sir William Curtis, but lost the election again in 1820, when he became sheriff; was Lord Mayor in 1823, and got into Parliament again in 1826. One can scarcely speak of Waithman's shop without referring to Hardham's, the famous tobacconist, at the sign of the Red Lion, next door but two. Hardham's celebrated " 37 " snuff was the rage in Garrick's time, partly because the great actor mentioned it on the stage, for Hardham had been Garrick's "numberer." Men of fashion as well as actors used to lounge at Hardham's, who made a large fortune. Various speculations have been made on the name " 37," given to the snuff, of which everybody took a pinch; but it has been said that it was simply the number on the drawer (37) in which it was kept. Hardham's was before Waithman's time, but it is pretty well remembered, as well almost as the negro sweeper who so long kept the clean crossing from Waithman's corner. For quaint reference this old "black" may be said to have succeeded the cobbler mentioned by Steele, whose stall was near the Bell Savage Gate, and who perhaps, being a rather cynical humourist, had standing by him the wooden figure of a man of fashion, "a swell," in the position of bowing, and so made as to hold in his hand the wax ends required by the old leather-stitcher in his business.

There were several noted shoeblacks in the locality, one of them also a negro; but the sweeper was, so to speak, a formidable rival to their trade, if, indeed, "Tim-buc-too," "Romeo," "Brutus Billy," for by these names he seems to have been known, could be antagonistic to any one. The name of this worthy old African was Charles M'Ghee, and he was the son of an old negro in Jamaica, who died at the age of 108. His short, rather clumsy figure, his grey hair, brushed up into a "brutus," or toupee, and his dress, composed of such decent but often incongruous cast-off garments as were given him, would be seen daily, no matter in what weather, at his "shop," as he called the crossing, from morning till dark, after which he took a basket, and sold nuts or oranges at the doors of a theatre or concert-room. He lived in a court near Drury Lane, and had the negro qualities of good humour and harmless fun, so that his anecdotes and remarks were often very amusing. It has been suggested that "Tim-buc-too" was the original "study" for the famous Billy Waters in *Tom and Jerry*, and of the "galanty" show drama. Miss Waithman was very kind to him, and often sent him out soup, bread, and other savoury meals, and at his death it was reported, but without authority, that he had left her a large sum of money (£7,000). That he made enough money to retire on in extreme old age there is little doubt, for retire he did, but not till he was very old, for his portrait at 73 was hung in the parlour of a tavern in Bride Lane. It is said, however, that he sold his crossing for a good round sum; though that is scarcely likely, for his successor was a soldier who got drunk, and, though he made sometimes as much as 8s. or 10s. a day, spent it in the evening. M'Ghee, or Brutus Billy, used to attend Rowland Hill's chapel, and lived to the age of 87, when he died in Chapel Court.

George Cruikskank must have gazed with delight at the queer figure of the negro sweeper, for at that time we find the successor of Hogarth and Rowlandson visiting the famous and once notorious satiriser and parodist, William Hone, at his shop at the corner of Ship Court, Old Bailey, or at the one he subsequently took on Ludgate Hill.

It would be impossible to record all that might be chronicled of the people who have been intimately associated with Ludgate Hill, even after the time that Dr. Johnson held his club in Ivy Lane, and Goldsmith wrote "Goody Twoshoes" for Mr. Newbery. It is difficult now to point out the exact spot occupied by shops and houses that were once historical, for the "march of improvement" does more than "Time's effacing finger," to destroy the old landmarks. There are *de*facements, too, as well as effacements, and the footprints come to be filled in with the

ROMAN REMAINS DISCOVERED ON LUDGATE HILL.

encroaching sand. If one could see what many of the shops were like, even at the end of the last century and at the beginning of this, we must abandon the idea of great panes of plate-glass, capacious vestibules, and ample show-rooms. That has not, even up to the present moment, been a characteristic of the Hill—the great London thoroughfare from West to East. But the shop-fronts were often picturesque with quaint carving, and there was a style about them not to be despised. On the north side, at No. 32, was Rundell & Bridge's, the royal goldsmiths and jewellers, with the sign of two golden salmon. Here was fitted up the crown for the coronation of George IV.* Many of us can remember Everington's shop, for the sale of sumptuous Oriental shawls, opposite; and there were others that are not yet forgotten, even though their successors have "room and verge enough" to represent the increased commercial activity of to-day. Ludgate Hill was not very many years ago considered to possess the finest shops in London, and it was here that the use of looking-glass, to reflect light and give a sense of space, was probably first used. It was on Ludgate Hill that the upper floor of a building was first taken into the shop so as to give height and room for displaying the goods, and the premises where this was done are now No. 69, immediately opposite where we are standing, at the corner of the Old Bell Savage.†

One other almost historic haunt must be mentioned, the "London Coffee House," which stood near Lud Gate and St. Martin's Church, and dates as a place of public entertainment from the days of George I., when it was noted for coffee, Dorchester beer, Welsh ale, and punch made in three different ways, and at a minute's notice, either with arrack, Jamaica rum, or French brandy. Later on, Rowley's cephalic snuff was sold here, and the London Coffee House was the resort of publishers, who held there the dinner at which they sold their copyrights. It stood in the liberties fo the Fleet, and had a passage to the Court-house of the Old Bailey, so that it became famous as the place where

* Mrs. Rundell wrote the once famous book on cookery.
† Once known as Harvey's, the linendraper's, but now occupied by Messrs. Treloar & Sons' carpet warehouse.

juries were taken during a trial, and there kept in snug quarters under the ward of an officer of the Court. This house was, in its later days, kept by the father of the famous John Leech, the artist of *Punch*, who was born there, and perhaps then acquired his early acquaintance with Londoners and their characteristics. It was in making some alterations at the back of the London Coffee House that several interesting relics of Roman London were discovered. In 1792, during some alterations in St. Martin's Court, the workmen came upon the remains of a barbican tower of the old City wall; and in the year 1806, at the back of the Coffee House, a singular tower and staircase was found, and three feet below the pavement the trunk of a statue of Hercules, half life-size, and a hexagonal altar or pedestal nearly 4 feet high and $2\frac{1}{2}$ feet wide, bearing an inscription which was deciphered to mean: "*Diis Manibus: Claudiæ Martinæ: Annorum XI. Anenclutus Provincialis Conjugi Pientissimæ hoc Sepulchrum (or hanc Statuam) erexit*"—a monument, in fact, to Claudina Martina, by her husband, a Roman soldier. A portion of a female head, life-size, was also discovered. On page 125 is an engraving representing these relics, and on the same page are engraved a Roman tile found at the foundation of the Post Office, St. Martin's-le-Grand in 1818 (Fig. 4); a small brass figure of Diana, $2\frac{1}{2}$ inches high, discovered between the Deanery of St. Paul's (in Doctors' Commons) and Blackfriars (Fig. 5); and a beautiful little silver figure of Harpocrates, $3\frac{1}{2}$ inches high, taken from some depth when digging for the foundation of new London Bridge (Fig. 6). The ring attached to the figure is of gold, and attached to a chain. At its feet are the figures of a dog, a tortoise, and a bird. It came into the possession of Messrs. Rundell & Bridge when it was found, in 1825, and they sent it from their shop in Ludgate Hill to the British Museum.

Conclusion.

And so we come down to the time when the London Coffee House was full of customers, and the Old Bell Savage —long ago altered to La Belle Sauvage—was still a flourishing inn, kept by Mr. Nelson, and known as a famous

COACH LEAVING BELL SAVAGE YARD.

coaching-house—the days, in fact, when the elder Mr. Weller drove from the Marquis of Granby at Dorking, and his son Sam was employed at that equally famous old inn in the Borough.

Even then the *mail coaches* assembled before the new Post Office nightly to carry the letters to the country, and it was not till the mail coach and the passenger coach had disappeared before the great railway system that the Belle Sauvage, along with many another good old inn, disappeared also. But the change is significant—as significant as the transformation of the great area, only part of which was occupied by the ancient hostelry, into the site of the vast building whence are issued books, magazines, and periodicals that carry information and instruction to every part of the globe.

When the London, Chatham and Dover Railway bought of the Corporation the ground made vacant by the destruction of the Fleet Prison, and it was known that the great flat iron bridge, with its snorting and shrieking traffic, was to shut out St. Paul's from the valley where the Fleet Ditch had been made into a part of the great drainage system, there were those who stood against so high-handed a claim; but the deed was done—

"A deed to shudder at, not to see;"

and to-day the engine pants and quivers on its way from the Holborn Viaduct to Ludgate Station, which occupies the space that once led steeply to the Blackfriars precinct. Beyond it are the stores of the great firm of refreshment purveyors who help to provide for that vast travelling public which is a mighty floating population; and still further is the great new bridge, built of vast and solid proportions from the designs of Mr. Cubitt, and completed in November 1869, when it was opened by our beloved sovereign—in one of those her rare visits to Ludgate Hill.

There are no shows and pageants now to adorn the bridge-foot or to climb the hill in honour of Royal visits; the people make the show, and the streets are filled with life. For the population has so increased that each decennial census is startling. It was computed more than twenty years ago that there passed through Ludgate Hill in twelve hours nearly 9,000 vehicles, above 13,000 horses, and about 106,000 persons; and it is certain that the number is vastly greater now, as may be judged by the following summary from a work called "Ten Years' Growth of the City of London," which gives the details of a day census taken on May 4th, 1891, by order of the Court of Common Council :—

PASSENGERS ON FOOT AND IN VEHICLES ENTERING THE CITY OF LONDON ON MAY 4TH, 1891.

In 16 Hours (Day), 5 a.m. to 9 p.m. 1,100,636
In 8 Hours (Night), 9 p.m. to 5 a.m. 85,458

TOTAL in 24 Hours (Day and Night), 5 a.m. to 5 a.m. 1,186,094

VEHICLES ENTERING THE CITY OF LONDON ON MAY 4TH, 1891.

In 16 Hours (Day), 5 a.m. to 9 p.m. 85,826
In 8 Hours (Night), 9 p.m. to 5 a.m. 6,546

TOTAL in 24 Hours (Day and Night), 5 a.m. to 5 a.m. 92,372

NUMBER AND DESCRIPTION OF VEHICLES ENTERING THE CITY OF LONDON ON MAY 4TH, 1891.

Cabs 18,020
Omnibuses 10,389
Other Four-wheeled Vehicles 42,366
Other two-wheeled Vehicles 21,597

Total No. of Vehicles ... 92,372

COMPARATIVE STATEMENT, 1881-1891.

Passengers.

	DAY TRAFFIC, 16 HOURS.	NIGHT TRAFFIC, 8 HOURS.	24 HOURS.
1881	739,640	57,923	797,563
1891	1,100,636	85,458	1,186,094

Vehicles.

	Cabs, Two and Four-wheeled.	Omnibuses.	Other Four-wheeled Vehicles.	Other Two-wheeled Vehicles.	Total Vehicles.
1881.					
16 Hours	14,042	5,326	28,244	19,297	66,909
8 Hours	1,924	850	1,152	1,058	4,984
24 Hours	15,966	6,176	29,396	20,355	71,893
1891.					
16 Hours	15,845	8,955	40,413	20,613	85,826
8 Hours	2,175	1,434	1,953	984	6,546
24 Hours	18,020	10,389	42,366	21,597	92,372

And yet London may, in a measure, be called the City of the Woods still, for there are yet bright patches of greenery about it, and trees are to be seen within the borders of the Ludgate district. There has lately been an anxious correspondence lest the fine plane-tree in Stationers' Hall Court should be cut down, and it is a pleasure to learn that no ruthless axe will lay it low to make room for "improvements." Nearly fifty years ago the esteemed treasurer of the Stationers' Company had it planted, and the "tree it still remains," flourishing yet; so flourishing that four may-trees planted in the corners of the Court had to be removed because the original tenant overshadowed them—so flourishing that two years ago a cuckoo was heard and seen in amidst its leafy covert—the same cuckoo, perhaps, which has this year been heard in that other noble tree at the corner of Wood Street, Cheapside. The garden of St. Paul's Churchyard is already growing apace fresh and green, and has become the midday and evening resort for the denizens of the great City. Children skip and play on the very spot where Paul's Cross once stood, with its dark memorials, and from a granite fountain the thirsty wayfarer may take a draught of water as sweet as ever ran from the conduit in Chepe. In Warwick Lane a new house of red brick and "modern mediæval" ornamentation is being built for the Canons of St. Paul's, and it may be hoped that there will be room for an academic grove there. On the other side, within Dean's Court, the deanery has its trees, trailing long green branches, and throwing cool shadows, and there is to be heard the cawing of rooks too—a sound, as old Pepys would say, "mighty pleasant"; while even in Addle Hill, and some of the adjacent lanes, we catch glimpses, not only of window-gardening and of climbing plants on string and trellis, but of veritable, goodly, tall trees, sometimes in strange and unexpected places. Nor can we do better than place this on record as one of the links that should serve to connect the Past and the Present of Ludgate Hill.

MODERN LUDGATE HILL WIDENED AND IMPROVED.

On September 27th, 1864, Lieut.-Colonel Haywood, the Engineer to the Commissioners of Sewers, brought up a report which stated that arrangements had been made with the London, Chatham, and Dover Railway Company, by which the Commissioners could, under certain conditions, purchase ground belonging to the Company, in order to increase the width of Ludgate Hill to sixty feet west of the point where the railway bridge was to cross the thoroughfare. Colonel Haywood submitted that this was a favourable opportunity for effecting a larger and more important improvement at that spot, so that the traffic which had become enormous might be divided, and danger dimished. By his plan he proposed to form a circus, 160 feet in diameter, and to erect a refuge or resting place in the centre, round which the traffic in each direction would pass. He said it was desirable that immediate action should be taken in the matter. On October 18th, 1864, the plan had been examined, the cost estimated, and the railway company had, through their solicitor, acceded to the terms for forming the eastern portion of the Circus at the foot of Ludgate Hill. The engineer subsequently stated that, according to the plan, an additional 17 feet of carriage way would be obtained, which would greatly facilitate traffic. The Chairman

THE PLANE-TREE IN STATIONERS' HALL COURT.

of the Commission proposed that the recommendation of the committee should be carried out, and stated that the estimated cost would be from £3,000 to £4,000. By the original plan for the railway bridge a footway was to be constructed beside the bridge, by which passengers might cross the hill without going on the roadway. The bridge was to be reached by an enclosed staircase on each side, in much the same manner as those which lead up to the Holborn Viaduct from Farringdon Street (the houses on each side of the road on Ludgate Hill have been set back for the purpose). Meanwhile the Committee of the Metropolitan Board of Works had decided to recommend to the Board to contribute half the money then required for further improvements on Ludgate Hill, the amount of such contribution being estimated at £11,756. This decision was imparted to the Court by Mr. Deputy Lowman Taylor, who at a subsequent meeting of the Commissioners, on February 25th, announced that the Board of Works had agreed to come to their assistance. This announcement was followed by what was practically the first step towards the promised improvements. Mr. (now Sir) J. Whittaker Ellis moving that notice should be immediately given under the powers of the Act of Parliament to take the whole of the premises at 57 and 59, Ludgate Hill, and property connected therewith; a motion which was seconded and carried. A very few plain figures will show that during the past 28 years, that is to say, since 1863, the rateable value of property on Ludgate Hill has more than doubled. In the parish of St. Gregory-by-St. Paul, which is on the north and south sides of Ludgate Hill from St. Paul's Churchyard to the centre of Ave Maria Lane and Creed Lane respectively, the gross value of the property in 1863 was £3,400; it is now £7,950. In St. Martin's, Ludgate, extending on the north side of the hill from the centre of Ave Maria Lane to the corner of Boy Court, and on the south side from the centre of Creed Lane to the east corner of Dolphin Court, the gross value in 1863 was £11,041; it is now £23,020. In St. Bride's parish the rateable value on Ludgate Hill in 1863 was £5,627; it is now £11,840. Thus the total amount in 1863 was £20,068, and it now is £42,810; the increase has therefore been £22,742. These figures to some extent indicate the cost of delay. But there was more than this. The policy which was adopted had the effect of allowing new interests to be created, and additional claims to be accumulated. The case of Goodman *v.* the Commissioners of Sewers, tried at Guildhall before the Recorder on April 29th, 1890, illustrated the manner in which claims for compensation were developed by the method of proceeding which had been adopted in relation to improvements on Ludgate Hill. The complainant in that case commenced, in 1885, to occupy premises on the south side of the hill, which should long before have been acquired for the extensions which were known to have been imminent. In February 1888 the Commissioners of Sewers gave notice that the premises would be wanted. In May 1889 Mr. Goodman obtained compensation for the compulsory removal. A month after this he secured other premises on the hill where there was sixteen years to run of a lease. None of the interests had been acquired by the Commissioners of Sewers, and no such notices had been given as might have barred the prosecution of a new claim by an occupier securing premises which were known to be on the line of demolition. The plaintiff had received substantial compensation in May, and removed to other premises in June. On July 3rd he again received notice to treat, and, not unnaturally, pleaded that he had again a substantial interest, and had incurred considerable expenses. The case was taken into Court, and Mr. Goodman was awarded £1,570. There is no need to expatiate on this case. It aptly illustrates the manner in which the cost of necessary improvements may be, and has been, enormously increased, and vindicates the action of those who, like myself, have made themselves troublesome by persistently pointing to the consequences of delay. Another announcement was made by Mr. Deputy Lowman Taylor, that the Committee of the Metropolitan Board of Works would recommend the Board to support the Commission in carrying out improvements, especially with regard to acquiring the house, 55, Ludgate Hill, to which they recommended a contribution of one-half the cost. Mr. Deputy Taylor represented that the

Board was "well alive to the fact that this was but a portion of the larger improvement then being contemplated," and he believed that the Board would readily assist in making the whole of the improvements on the south side.

The London County Council has repudiated the arrangements made by its predecessor, the Metropolitan Board of Works, to pay a proportion of the cost of this great improvement. When stating this it is as well to call attention to the fact, that during the past thirty-eight years the Commission of Sewers has expended out of the consolidated rate of the City a gross sum of £3,900,000 for improvements. Towards this the Metropolitan Board of Works has contributed something like £591,000, which amount, together with that received by the Commission for the sale of surplus lands, etc., amounting to £1,121,000, leaves a sum approaching £2,188,000 spent by the Commission for improvements in the City since the year 1850. In addition to this large expenditure, it must be borne in mind that the City of London pays annually about one-eighth of the entire cost of all the improvements in the Metropolis effected by the London County Council. It must also be borne in mind that the great bulk of this expenditure has not been made for mere local improvements, for they embrace every main street in the City, through which passes, in the aggregate, the largest traffic in the world. The City improvements are, in fact, for the most part made for the benefit and convenience of the entire Metropolis, and not alone for the City of London. There is not a part of the Metropolis which does not add its quota of traffic to the 1,864,094 of people and 92,000 vehicles which enter and leave the City of London daily.

At a meeting held on September 10th, 1878, Mr. (now Deputy) Bedford effectively awakened the Commission to further action by calling attention to the fact that no fewer than six properties on the south side were being rebuilt, and if this opportunity were lost none such might occur again. He moved a resolution in accordance with his forcible speech, and was seconded by Mr. Hicks, who declared that if they lost this opportunity they would regret it but once—and that would be for ever. Mr. Deputy

Lowman Taylor again said, that if the works were undertaken the Metropolitan Board of Works would give them aid. The matter was referred to a committee, and in a few days it was agreed to take the six properties referred to. In 1882, when the late Mr. John Cox was chairman of the Finance Committee, the subject was again brought forward, and Mr. Hicks and Mr. Shaw both advocated immediate action, the last named gentleman presenting a petition from the inhabitants praying for the improvement to be completed.

On October 9th, 1883, Mr. Deputy Cox moved that notice be served to take the several interests in the premises 27, 29, and 31, and the motion, seconded by Mr. Morton, and supported by Mr. Felton, who declared "that the state of Ludgate Hill was an eyesore to every one," was carried. In January 1885 Mr. Judd called the attention of the Commission of Sewers to the continued delay in the improvement. He truly said that people occupying premises there had suffered for years, and that many of them had become bankrupt through the still existing disorder. On February 23rd of this year, 1885, I presented a petition from the inhabitants asking that immediate steps be taken to pull down the remaining houses. The memorial bore the signature of one hundred and ten firms. I moved to comply with the prayer of the petition, and was supported by Mr. (now Alderman) Green and Mr. Shaw; but this was not carried, and the question was deferred until November 1887, when I again moved that the usual notice should be served to acquire the leasehold of 37, 39, 41, 45, and 47; this motion was seconded by Mr. C. Mathew, and supported by Mr. Deputy Cox, Mr. Judd, Mr. Alderman Lawrence, and Mr. Alderman Gray, and carried. On June 18th, 1889, I moved "that it be referred to the Finance Committee to consider the question of taking immediate steps for completing the improvement of Ludgate Hill"; this was seconded by Mr. MacGeagh, Mr. Deputy Walter, and others.

In this year, 1889, a proposal was made to open up St. Martin's Court to vehicular traffic, by increasing its width to twenty-five feet. If this had been agreed to the most valuable site on Ludgate Hill, now occupied by the new premises of the City Bank, would have been given up.

The rental of the ground is £2,200. The improvement, if any, was not necessary, as the roadway, when made, would have led only to a narrow lane. On February 10th, 1891, I was fortunate enough to induce the Commissioners of Sewers to pass a resolution, which practically completed the widening of Ludgate Hill. Of course the matter was referred to on many other occasions than those I have mentioned, but it would be nothing but "damnable iteration" to mention every time that attention was called to Ludgate Hill. The total length of the thoroughfare is 850 feet, the width, which was formerly 47 feet, is now 60 feet, and the total net cost to the City has been about £325,000.

I desire to place on record that, though I have received most gratifying expressions of the appreciation of my neighbours for the efforts I have been able to make in this matter, I do not claim any credit for the result. Others, as I have endeavoured to show, have been quite as anxious as myself to complete this movement. Mr. Salmon, in his admirable book, "Ten Years' Growth of the City of London," tells us that "either further improvements in the streets must be made, or the City will become inadequate to the requirements of its business." I quite agree with this remark, and think a very useful further improvement might be made by throwing open the north side of St. Paul's Churchyard to vehicular traffic; this, I believe, may be done at a trifling cost by removing the railings and making some slight alterations. In the year 1868 the Metropolitan Board of Works considered that this would be desirable, and negotiations with this object were accordingly entered into by the Commission of Sewers with the Dean and Chapter of St. Paul's. The Cathedral authorities, however, objected to the proposal, and therefore no action was taken in the matter. Meantime, it is consolatory to think that it did not take much more than a quarter of a century to accomplish by degrees the widening of Ludgate Hill.

INDEX.

Addle Hill, 134.
Addle Lane, 93.
Admiralty Court, The, 63.
Alleyn, the actor, 57.
Alms for prisoners, 45, 113.
Amen Corner, 43, 69, 71, 93.
Ancient taverns in St. Paul's Churchyard, 93, 94.
Apothecaries' Hall, 81.
Ave Mary Lane, 30, 37, 43, 69, 93.
Ballium, or Bailey, The, 47.
Bankes, and his horse, 12, 67, 68.
Barclay, the Quaker, and George III., 99.
"Barnaby Rudge," Graphic description of City life in, 111.
Bartholomew Fair, 29, 72.
Baynard's Castle, 12, 21; incidents in its history, 24—29.
"Bell Savage" Inn, 10, 46, 52, 55, 67, 68, 119; origin of the name, 46; view of, 91; coach leaving the, 129; the Belle Sauvage Works, 127.
Bell Tavern, Old Bailey, 66.
Ben Jonson, 12, 29, 58, 72, 82.
Black Friars, The, 20, 49.
Blackfriars Bridge, 115; the new bridge, 131.
Blackfriars Theatre, 29, 30, 57.
Booksellers, Famous, 83, 87, 90, 93.
Booksellers' shops in the olden time, 90.
Bowyer Row, 30, 43, 44.
Breakneck Steps, 108.
Bridewell, 11, 20, 21—23, 56, 73, 95, 110.
Bullies and roysterers in the streets, 83, 116.
Burbage, the actor, 12, 57, 72.
Burgavenny House, 70.
Canon Alley, 93.
Cemetery, Discovery of the site of a, 18.
Central Criminal Court, 108.
Chapter Coffee House, The, 93.
City Watch, The, 48.
Coaches, Use of, 57, 76.
Cocker, the arithmetician, 34.
Cold Harbour House, 65.
College of Arms (*see* Heralds' College).

College of Physicians, 18, 71, 81.
College of Surgeons, 82.
Creed Lane, 37, 43, 93.
Cuckoo, The, on Ludgate Hill, 133.
Dance of Death, 46.
Dangers of the streets, 83, 84, 116.
Darkness of the old streets, 48.
Dean's Court, 134.
De Keyser's Hotel, 21.
Derby House, 66.
Diana Chamber, The, 33.
Diana, Supposed Temple of, on the site of St. Paul's, 15, 33.
Doctors' Commons, 31, 62, 63, 64.
Do-Little Lane, 93.
Dolly's Tavern, 94.
Drake, Sir Francis, 12, 53, 54.
Dugdale, Sir W., 65.
Durham House, 65.
Eldernesse Lane, 44.
Erkenwald, the Saxon saint, 18, 34, 42.
Everington, Messrs., 127.
Executions at Newgate, Number of, 107, 108.
Farringdon Market, 114.
Fire, the Great, 64, 65, 70, 71, 72, 76, 80, 84, 87.
Fitzwalter, Robert, 24, 25.
Fleet Bridge, 11, 20, 73, 95.
Fleet Ditch, 20, 73, 82, 105; view of the, 106.
Fleet Lane, 20.
Fleet Market, 105, 114; illustration of, 103.
Fleet parsons and marriages, 100—105; illustration of, 103.
Fleet Prison, 11, 56, 76, 100, 110; some account of, 110—114; abolition and demolition of, 114.
Fleet Street, 16, 72, 120.
Fleet, The River, 11, 16, 18, 19, 20, 21; its stagnant condition, 21.
Foot-passengers in the streets, Dangers of, 82.
Forster, Robert, and the widow, 45.
Funeral sermon, a curious, 23.
George III.'s visit to St. Paul's, 115.
Gibbons, Grinling, the wood-carver, 119.

INDEX. 143

Giltspur Street Compter, 29.
Godliman Street, 34.
Goldsmith, Oliver, 82, 108, 124.
Green Arbour Court, Old Bailey, 108.
Gunpowder Plot conspirators, The, 72.
Guy Fawkes Processions on Ludgate Hill, 87.
Hardham's snuff-shop, 123.
Harvey, the physician, 71.
Hatton, Sir Christopher, 62, 63.
Hebrew inscription found on Ludgate Hill, 26.
Heralds' College, or College of Arms, 65, 66.
Hoadley, Bishop, 70.
Hogarth, 94, 95.
Holborn Bridge, 21, 105.
Holborn Viaduct, 114.
Hone, the bookseller, 124.
Horn Lanterns, Illuminations by, 48.
Inigo Jones, 64, 73, 74.
Inns of London, formerly the mansions of the nobility, 56.
Ivy Lane, 124.
James I., 70—72.
Johnson, Dr., 93, 115, 124.
King John, 24.
King Lud, 13, 15, 110; effigy of, 14.
Kings-at-Arms, Eminent, 66.
King's Printing House, The, 32.
Knightrider Street, 44, 62, 71.
La Belle Sauvage Inn, 128.
Lollards' Tower, 43.
London Coffee House, The, 127, 128.
London, Derivation of, 15, 17.
London House Yard, 38.
Longmans', Messrs., 90.
Looking-glass, Use of, on Ludgate Hill, 127.
Lord Mayor's Show, 95—100; Hogarth's sketch of a, 97.
Lud Gate, 11, 13, 38, 75, 80, 127; view of, 16; its appearance during the great fire, 80; demolition of, 110.
Ludgate Hill: a retrospective sketch, 9—11; Roman and other relics found on, 17, 18; the feudal period, 19, 21, 22; Queen Elizabeth on, 49—54; after the fire, 76; views of, 85, 121; royal and other processions on, 72, 87, 117; its former shops and shopfronts, 123, 124; old view of, 118; present appearance of, *Frontispiece*; the railway bridge, 131; daily traffic over, 131.
Ludgate Prison, 43, 110.
Madam Creswell and her funeral sermon, 23.
Mail-coaches on Ludgate Hill, 131.
Marriages at the Fleet Prison, 100—105.
Matrimonial and Wills Courts, 63.
M'Ghee, the negro shoeblack, 123, 124.

Mohocks, and other street ruffians, 84, 116.
Mrs. Salmon's waxwork, 73.
Mylne, the architect, 89, 115.
Narrow streets, Difficulty in traversing the, 82; darkness of the, 84.
Newbery, the bookseller, 93, 124.
Newgate Calendar, The, 107.
Newgate Market, 44, 71.
Newgate Prison, 44, 56, 76, 107; executions at, 107, 108, 109.
Nonconformist meeting-houses, Attack on, 89.
"No Popery" riots, 111, 115.
Nos. 68 and 69, Ludgate Hill, 12, 127.
Oil Lamps, First use of, 116.
Old Bailey, The, 71, 82, 108, 109.
Old Bourne, The, or Holborn, 16, 20.
Old Change, 37, 93.
Old Houses on Ludgate Hill, 48, 49.
Old London Wall, Ludgate Hill, View of, 121.
Old Moore's Almanack, 69.
Old St. Paul's, 10, 33—43; site of the old building, 34; view of, 35; its dimensions, 37; its historical associations, 37—43; a public promenade and a common thoroughfare for merchandise, 59, 61; its renovation by Inigo Jones, 73.
Pardon Church, 46.
Paternoster Row, 37, 43, 68, 90; silkmercers and lacemen, its former residents, 84.
Paul's Bakehouse, 34.
Paul's Brewhouse, 34.
Paul's Chain, 33, 34.
Paul's Cross, 27, 37.
Paul's Gate, 30.
Paul's Head Tavern, 34.
"Paul's Walkers," 61.
Paul's Wharf, 21, 29, 33.
Peace of Ryswick, 87, 88.
Pembroke Inn, 43, 70.
"Pickwick Papers," 112, 114.
"Pitt Bridge," 115.
Pitt, Mr., Enthusiastic reception of, 100.
Plague, The, in the City, 60, 72, 75.
Plane-tree, The, in Stationers' Hall Court, Illustration of, 135.
Players at the "Bell Savage," 55, 56.
Playhouse Yard, 12.
Prerogative Will Office, 63.
Printing House Square, 31.
Processions and pageants on Ludgate Hill, 28, 49—54, 87, 89, 96—100, 117.
Public games in the open streets, 83.
Puddle Dock, 21, 29, 30.
Puddle Dock Hill, 30.
Puddle Wharf, 30.
Purchas, Samuel, 80.
Queen Anne, Ludgate Hill in the time of, 87; her statue, 90.

INDEX.

Queen Catherine, Trial of, 22.
Queen Elizabeth on Ludgate Hill, 49—54.
Queenhithe, 30, 31.
Queen's Head Tavern, Paternoster Row, 63.
Remarkable Wills in Doctors' Commons, 63.
Restoration, Gay doings in honour of the, 74.
Ridley, Bishop, 22.
River of Wells, The, 16, 20.
Roman relics and remains, 17, 18, 20, 128; illustration of, 125.
Roman Wall, The old, 17, 18, 128.
Royal Wardrobe, The, 21, 30, 31, 32; some account of, 31.
Rundell & Bridge, Messrs., 127, 128.
Sacheverel, Dr., Riots on account of, 88, 89.
St. Andrew in the Wardrobe, 30, 31.
St. Andrew's Hill, 21, 30.
St. Bartholomew's Hospital, 44, 56.
St. Bennet's Hill, 62, 65.
St. Bridget's Well, 11, 21.
St. Cecilia's Feast, 70.
St. Faith's Church, 38, 87.
St. Gregory's Church, St. Paul's, 38, 45.
St. Martin's, Ludgate, 71, 80.
St. Martin's Court, Remains of the old City wall in, 128; illustration of, 121.
St. Michael le Querne, Paternoster Row, 30.
St. Michael's Church, Queenhithe, 30.
St. Paul's Cathedral (*see also* Old St. Paul's): completion of Wren's edifice, 89; cost of, 90; George III.'s visit to, 117.
St. Paul's Churchyard: amusements formerly practised in, 75; its shape, 93; trees in, 133.
St. Paul's Coffee-house, 34.
St. Paul's School, 56, 67.
St. Peter's College, 69.
Saxon remains, 18.
Seacole Lane, 108.
Sedan Chairs, Use of, 59, 82.
Sermon Lane, 93.
Shakespeare, 12, 26, 27, 29, 54, 55, 56, 57, 67, 72; his will, 29, 63.
Ship Court, Old Bailey, 124.
Shops in St. Paul's Churchyard, 74.

Sidney, Sir Philip, 53, 62.
Signboards, The old, 83, 84, 123.
Stalls or booths on Ludgate Hill, 60, 74.
Star Chamber and the Blackfriars Theatre, 58.
Stationers' Company, The, 69.
Stationers' Hall, 68—71.
Stationers' Hall Court, The Plane-tree in, 133—135.
Stationers, Locality formerly occupied by, 32.
Surgeons' Hall, 82, 107.
Swift, Dean, 82, 94.
Tarleton, the jester, 12, 68.
Taverns and inns near Ludgate Hill, 94.
Taylor, the water poet, 58, 59.
Thames, The, 12, 16, 18, 33, 51.
Theatrical performances in the olden time, 56, 68.
Thieves and robbers, 83, 84; haunts of, 105.
Tim-buc-too, the crossing-sweeper, 120.
Times newspaper, The, 33.
Trees in the City, 131, 133, 134.
Treloar & Sons, 12, 127.
Troynovant, the old city of, 14.
Tudor sovereigns, The, 26, 27, 46—54, 72.
Turkey carpets, Use of, 50, 87.
Waithman, Alderman, 119—123; obelisk in honour of, 120.
Walsingham, Sir Francis, 62.
Wardrobe Court, 31.
Waterworks at London Bridge, 75.
Warwick House, 44.
Warwick Inn, 44.
Warwick Lane, 44, 71, 134.
"Warwick Roll," The, 66.
Weapon show, 44.
Weller, Sam, 34, 131.
Whitefriars, 73.
White Friars, The, 20.
Wilkes and the *North Briton*, 100; obelisk in honour of, 115.
William III., Ludgate Hill in the time of, 87.
Wren, Sir Christopher, 18, 31, 89; and St. Martin's Church, 80; his plan for rebuilding of the City after the Fire, 79, 80; his poetical monument, 90.
Wyatt's Rebellion, 12, 51, 52.

Printed by Hazell, Watson, & Viney, Ld., London and Aylesbury.

www.ingramcontent.com/pod-product-compliance
Lightning Source LLC
Chambersburg PA
CBHW030354170426
43202CB00010B/1375